EDUCATION AND RELIGION

EDUCATION AND RELIGION

The Bedell Lectures for 1926-27

And Other Addresses on Construction and Reconstruction in Education

BY

CHARLES FRANKLIN THWING

Essay Index Reprint Series

BOOKS FOR LIBRARIES PRESS
FREEPORT, NEW YORK

First Published 1929
Reprinted 1970

STANDARD BOOK NUMBER:
8369-1629-8

LIBRARY OF CONGRESS CATALOG CARD NUMBER:
71-105044

PRINTED IN THE UNITED STATES OF AMERICA

PREFATORY NOTE

THIS volume begins with four lectures given in Kenyon College in the year 1926-27 on the Bedell Foundation. This Foundation was laid in the year 1880 by Bishop and Mrs. Bedell for the purpose of interpreting religion both natural and revealed, and also for examining the relations of science and religion.

The remaining chapters are addresses which, in the course of almost forty years, I have given at college commencements and convocations, at meetings of medical and legal societies, and before other associations. In a sense they intimate the thinkings of a college president through the tenth decade of the last, and the first three decades of the present, century.

CHARLES F. THWING

CONTENTS

EDUCATION AND RELIGION

EDUCATION AND RELIGION

I

EDUCATION AND RELIGION AS EXPERIENCE

In the beginning I wish my first word to be one of thankfulness. For, the opportunity of serving upon this historic Foundation, the privilege of standing in a great succession of churchmen and of college leaders, command my deep gratitude.

The subject which I have chosen for the course is Education and Religion: their correspondence or correlation. With your indulgence, I shall speak upon the theme in four relations; first, as experience; second, as form and content; third, as forces appealing to the reason and other faculties; and fourth, in conclusion, as forces calling for development, and consummation or fruitage.

The selection of this theme requires no defense. For, of all places in America, Kenyon represents the union of the forces of education and of religion in a degree most impressive. For a hundred and more years, the church, as the exponent of religion, and the college, as the organ of the higher education, have here coöperated in noble efficiency, and unto the richest results.

By religion, as I shall constantly use the word, I refer

specifically to the Christian faith, of which the organ is the church. But, at times, I may use the word in a yet broader meaning. For religion represents the relationship which man holds to Ultimate Being. It includes Ultimate Being itself, it includes man, it includes the process or medium which unites the object and the subject. The common interpretation of the word supports such a meaning—the binding of man to his God. For religion does stand for those ties which unite God and man. Another definition, recognized by Murray, derived from Cicero, makes the word stand for reading, or rereading, as if, through religion, man came to understand the divine. But, at all events, the definition which I have ventured to impose, the relation which man holds to Ultimate Being, has good support.

In my interpretation of education, nothing recondite is to be found. I shall, however, on the whole, limit the word to what is called the higher education, the collegiate foundation, its form, structure, method, and fulfillment.

In this lecture I shall seek to present education and religion as a personal experience.

Experience stands for the learning, the forgetting, the thinking, the feeling, the rejoicing and the suffering, the hoping and the despairing, the accepting and the refusing, of the individual man. It refers to the phenomena which belong to or are incarnated in the person. It means life lived. It is contrasted with the ideal, the imaginative, the remote. It may be, or it may not be, humanistic. But it is human. It belongs to man as man.

It pertains to him as the subject, the object, of all the states and of all the conditions which help to constitute him as a member of the race. In my boyhood in the State of Maine, the phrase was often used, "experiencing religion." It was sometimes used as a question, "Have you experienced religion?" A very personal question it was, asked by one who was anxious about the soul of a friend, whose spiritual state might be doubtful. The question meant, and still means, Has the Christian faith become vital, real, formative, constructive in you? The same form might be quite as fittingly used as applied to education, Have you experienced education? Has education become a vital, real, formative, constructive force in you? The philosopher may phrase experience in a different way. Professor Gardiner, of Smith College, has recently defined it "As a whole in terms of concrete categories, humanizing the physical facts by viewing them in relation to mind and objectifying the facts of mind by viewing them as functions through which the individual realizes his unity with nature and with his fellow-men." [1]

For, both education and religion are, alike, forces for and of experience. The subject to be evangelized, the subject to be educated, is a person. It is neither the unsentient stone, nor the unreasoning, the unethical, unreligious brute which is concerned. The subject is the person. The person performing all acts which are deemed intellectual, the person feeling all the moods which we connote as emotional, the person appreciating

[1] *Philosophical Review*, July, 1926, p. 367.

the states which we name aesthetic, the person making all choices which belong to freedom, the person the object of remorse or of exultation—the person is the subject of experience. The subject is the person who seeks, as he is able, to know God and all spiritual phenomena. The person is he who follows after God, if haply and happily he may find Him. The person is he who chooses or rejects whatever he regards as the right. The person is he who rejoices in, or who is indifferent to, or antagonistic to, the true, the good, and the beautiful. The subject, therefore, who is evangelized and the subject who is educated are, alike, the person. The function performed by the church through its priesthood, and the function performed by the university through its teachers, are alike personal. Emerson says in one of his early essays: "A man, a personal ascendency, is the only great phenomenon. When Nature has work to be done, she creates a genius to do it. Follow the great man, and you shall see what the world has at heart in these ages. There is no omen like that. But what strikes us in the fine genius is that which belongs of right to every one." [2] But one can change the phrases and strengthen their meaning. For, it is not simply the genius, the great man, with whom one is concerned, but with every man, and not with the man in these ages, but with every man of every age. Man the person is the one who is the subject and the object of both religion and of education.

[2] *The Method of Nature: Nature, Addresses and Lectures,* by Ralph Waldo Emerson (Cambridge edition), Vol. I, p. 207.

But the person is not only the subject and the object of religion and education in human experience. He is also the agent who forms and reforms, establishes and reëstablishes, interprets and reinterprets, vitalizes and projects both education and religion as necessary and essential. For, both are apostolic; both are missionary. Each has its apostles, as each has its learners. Each gathers from the other and for the other. Certain truths of the gospels are illustrated in the Dialogues of Plato. In Raphael's school at Athens, Plato stands for the heaven-born philosophy, as Aristotle represents the more materialistic conception. Likewise, consider the influence of a single mind on religion and on the church, St. Augustine. Think of him as a theologian, as an administrator, the greatest of the four fathers of the Latin church, more philosophic than Ambrose, more saintly than Jerome, more outstanding than Gregory. As Principal Tulloch says of him, "No single name has ever exercised such power over the Christian church, and no one mind ever made such an impression upon Christian thought." [3] If one wished to go further afield in seeking for the power of the person influencing theological thought and ecclesiastical order, one would pause before the name of Martin Luther. Luther, the union of impetuosities and of courage, of intellectual eccentricities and of philosophic soundness, of ignorance and of distinguished learning, of narrowness and of breadth, of immediate rights and insights, and of far-off visions—how profound, how lasting, is that

[3] *The Encyclopædia Britannica* (9th ed.), Vol. III, p. 75.

influence over Christian faith, and over the higher education!

The power of personality for making experience in both education and religion is quite as fully and forcibly illustrated in our own time as in any preceding age. I first turn to one who embodies, on the side of religion, the inexpressible worth of personality. Phillips Brooks, in his Yale Lectures, you recall, interprets the preacher as having two forces or conditions. They are personality and truth, personality setting forth the truth, and truth as incarnated in, and expressed by personality.

> Even if [said Brooks] we look at preaching only, it must still be true that nothing can ever take its place because of the personal element that is in it. No multiplication of books can ever supercede the human voice. No newly opened channel of approach to man's mind and heart can ever do away with man's readiness to receive impressions through his fellow-man. There is no evidence, I think, in all the absorption in books which characterizes our much reading age, of any real decline of the interest in preaching. Let a man be a true preacher, really uttering the truth through his own personality, and it is strange how men will gather to listen to him. We hear that the day of the pulpit is past, and then some morning the voice of a true preacher is heard in the land and all the streets are full of men crowding to hear him, just exactly as were the streets of Constantinople when Chrysostom was going to preach at the Church of the Apostles, or the streets of London when

> Latimer was bravely telling his truth at St. Paul's.[4]
>
> However the Gospel may be capable of statement in dogmatic form, its truest statement we know is not in dogma but in personal life. Christianity is Christ; and we can easily understand how a truth which is of such peculiar character that a person can stand forth and say of it "I am the Truth," must always be best conveyed through, must indeed be almost incapable of being perfectly conveyed except through personality.[5]

How nobly Brooks illustrates all that he has just said, in himself. How forceful he was, yet how tender; how loving, yet how indignant at wrong. How fully he gave himself, yet ever finding more, the more he gave. How tolerant, yet how loyal; how grand his sweep of thought, yet how helpful to the individual person, his mind broad as the ocean and his heart as deep; how individualistic, yet how responsive unto all. In Brooks were united the contradictories. He was the great preacher because he was the great personality. As a great personality, he gave himself to religion. As I write, a picture of him hangs at my side. He was my preacher for the years of my education. But he was my preacher because, in part at least, he was my man, my friend.

[4] *The Two Elements in Preaching:* Lectures on Preaching, before the Divinity School of Yale College, 1877, by Phillips Brooks, pp. 11-12.

[5] *Ibid.*, p. 7.

A similar power of experience for education, and for a like reason, lies in a great teacher. Great teachers are great because they are first great persons. You can select the foremost teachers of any age. From our own age, I draw examples, just naming them—Mark Hopkins of Williams, Garman of Amherst, Sumner of Yale, Henry Adams, James, and Palmer of Harvard.

Religion and education are not only an experience for the person, as a subject and as an agent; they are also an experience in respect to what may be called a biographical or personal origin. Religion, or religious experience, for the person, begins with the birth, in, and for, and from, God. That beginning is called by different names. It is sometimes called conversion, as if one were turning away from the old and into the new. It is sometimes called the new birth, a birth out of an old into a new life. The one word, regeneration, in a technical way, expresses the meaning. But all the phrases agree in Christ's interpretation, recorded in the third chapter of the Gospel of St. John. One must be born from above, or through God—ἄνωθεν—or born a second time—δεύτερον. This birth may be unconscious, or it may be the process and the result of a mighty struggle and striving. It may be cyclonic, beginning almost in revulsions and convulsions. Of course, the stormier form is the more typical in Christian biography. If one wish for examples, let him turn to James' *Varieties of Religious Experience.* Many and diverse are the illustrations which are thus offered in the Gifford Lectures of the great psychologist. I venture to make mention of a single experience in the early life of Finney, so long a president of an historic Ohio college:

> All my feelings seemed to rise and flow out; and the utterance of my heart was, "I want to pour my whole soul out to God." The rising of my soul was so great that I rushed into the room back of the front office, to pray.
>
> There was no fire, and no light, in the room; nevertheless it appeared to me as if it were perfectly light. As I went in and shut the door after me, it seemed as if I met the Lord Jesus Christ face to face. It did not occur to me then, nor did it for some time afterward, that it was wholly a mental state. On the contrary it seemed to me that I saw him as I would see any other man. He said nothing, but looked at me in such a manner as to break me right down at his feet. I have always since regarded this as a most remarkable state of mind; for it seemed to me reality, that he stood before me, and I fell down at his feet and poured out my soul to him. I wept aloud like a child, and made such confessions as I could with my choked utterance. It seemed to me that I bathed his feet with my tears; and yet I had no distinct impression that I touched him, that I recollect.
>
> I must have continued in this state for a good while; but my mind was too much absorbed with the interview to recollect anything I said. But I know, as soon as my mind became calm enough to break off from the interview, I returned to the

front office, and found that the fire that I had made of large wood was nearly burned out. But as I turned and was about to take a seat by the fire, I received a mighty baptism of the Holy Ghost. Without any expectation of it, without ever having the thought in my mind that there was any such thing, . . . the Holy Spirit descended upon me in a manner that seemed to go through me, body and soul. I could feel the impression, like a wave of electricity, going through and through me. Indeed, it seemed to come in waves and waves of liquid love; for I could not express it in any other way. It seemed like the very breath of God. I can recollect distinctly that it seemed to fan me, like immense wings.

No words can express the wonderful love that was shed abroad in my heart. I wept aloud with joy and love; and I do not know but I should say, I literally bellowed out the unutterable gushings of my heart. These waves came over me, and over me, and over me, one after the other, until I recollect I cried out, "I shall die if these waves continue to pass over me." I said, "Lord, I cannot bear any more"; yet I had no fear of death.[6]

An experience so fundamental is not indeed usual. The more common is of the type belonging to Samuel, called out of his boyhood's longings to be a priest of God. And also more common is the experience of David, going from his sheepfold to become a singer and a king.

[6] *Memoirs of Rev. Charles G. Finney. Written by Himself*, pp. 19-21.

In our own immediate time, and in the typical American college of Christian foundation, an instance of the new birth is recorded in the experience of Stanley Hall. The great psychologist says:

> Near the end of my sophomore year, in the usual spring revival, two seniors whom I greatly respected began to cultivate my acquaintance and urge upon me the importance of "taking a stand for Christ." They even insisted on praying for me in my room and finally conducted me to a prayer meeting, and when the leader asked all who desired to be saved to rise, both of them—one on each side—urged me to stand, which I finally did with great reluctance. This, in that day and place meant that I was suffering from conviction of sin, and accordingly, by various stages which I do not recall in detail, I was led to believe that I had been converted. The next fall I united with the college church and for the two remaining years attended and sometimes took part in the various prayer meetings—class, college, etc. As I look back upon this I cannot think that it made any great change in my life although it did bring me into certain new associations and gave my parents great joy. I do not think that my emotional experiences were very deep. If they were, I do not remember them.[7]

For my present purpose, the value of these instances is largely comparative. Experiences not dissimilar have

[7] *Life and Confessions of a Psychologist,* by G. Stanley Hall, p. 163.

occurred in the life of many a college man, in respect to his intellect. The experiences may be tumultuous, cyclonic, or they may be as the still small voice, or the breath of the vesper breeze. But there is in the intellect of man, as well as in his heart and will, a new birth. It is to this new birth in education that I ask your thought.

There comes a time in the life of most persons of intellectual tastes and conditions when the powers of thought and reason take on forces mightier and larger than were before possessed, employed, or recognized. These persons spring from intellectual boyhood or girlhood to intellectual maturity. They put away childish things. So great is the change that it may be fittingly called the intellectual new birth or the intellectual second birth. It is a change in which the powers outside of themselves which make for thought unite with the powers within themselves which make for thought. The result is a new life, a new being, a creature unlike the old, and yet one with the old. It intimates Kant's dictum—the identity or unity of self-consciousness.

There is no set year for the beginning of this new life. Like the new birth, to which I have referred, it may come without observation; it may come like the spiritual regeneration, before the years of consciousness. Some natures are intellectually alert and vigorous from the very beginning. It may occur gradually, stealing over the spirit with the quiet and steady pace of the rising of the sun; and the man may in some crisis of his being find himself of a vision broader and of an inspiration keener than of old. It may come suddenly. I know instances of this new birth that deserve to be compared with some cataclysm of nature, so startling, so revolutionary are they, in process and in result. In one important way they differ from the cataclysm of nature, for the new birth is always constructive. It may also be said that in certain men the intellectual new birth never occurs. One may never reach his conscious intellectual life, and his possibilities never become potencies. The flesh may permanently dominate the mind. The spark of the mind may be buried and put out in the physical mass. That which is designed to be the expression of the mind and also the tool and the agent of the mind, the body, may usurp the functions of its proper master, the mind, and the spirit is lost in the flesh. But in most persons the intellectual life does come to its arousing, enlargement, and enrichment.

Although there is no set year for this awakening, yet in most persons the awakening comes between the years of seventeen and twenty-one. It occurs in the college age. In the college age, that time which falls in the middle of the course represents the usual hour of ripening. College officers frequently observe a great and vital difference between the sophomore and the junior. The boy or girl, a sophomore, is juvenile; the sophomore boy or girl become a junior, is mature! In a few months the man seems to have found his soul. He has come to himself. He has found himself. He is born again. He lives!

I recall a striking instance of this character. A man

whom I shall call Mr. Angel came to college from a home of culture. His bearing indicated ability. The first two years of his course were largely idle years. Without severe work he maintained a fairly respectable standing in his class. Near the close of his sophomore year he discussed the question of leaving college and taking up the study of music. For some reason or other he decided to continue. With the opening of the junior year appeared a man quite different from the man who said good-bye to his classmates at the close of the sophomore year. His step had become more vigorous, the expression of his face more alert and spirited. Idleness was transformed into laboriousness. Vigorous power of every sort was manifested in the man. Vigor and power of every sort were more and more manifested in the man in the following two years. One could almost see the man grow from week to week. His conversation became larger, richer; the relations of his thought world-wide. At the close of his course he pronounced one of the best addresses ever given on the Commencement platform. In the week following graduation he sailed for Germany, where he spent three years in study, and at the conclusion he received the doctor's degree with *Magna cum Laude.*

The evidences of this change are usually not recondite. Not seldom the body suggests the change: the eye takes on a brighter brightness; the face becomes more alert. Even, at times, a new light may seem to be shining forth from it. The bearing indicates increasing individuality, enlarging personality. But there are evidences more significant than any physical changes.

This awakening intellect is characterized by the spirit of inquiry. Its mood is interrogative. This spirit of inquiry touches the inner world of itself and the outer world. It is at once philosophic and scientific. Its first field of investigation is usually its own nature. It asks, What am I? It searches out the validity of its own possessions, mental, emotional, volitional. It asks, What is truth? and, unlike Pilate, is usually willing to wait for an answer. Nay, it seeks to make answer for itself. It casts its light into the depths of the human heart, seeking for the things which deserve affection. It forces its way into the citadel of the human will and begs to know the truth as to the supreme attributes of human destiny. It applies its questions to the human conscience. It tries the mysteries of remorse and approbation. All that psychology conveys to us about man the awakened intellect seeks to know of the individual himself. When it is aroused, its mood is one of full self-examination.

A further evidence of this awakening nature is seen in its self-confidence. It believes in itself. It is egotistic in the most worthy sense and also in a sense that may not be the most worthy. This confidence in himself arises from the man discovering in himself powers of which he had no intimation as existing. He finds himself stronger, larger, richer than he thought. This self-confidence may be quiet or expressive, modest or haughty, as respects the motive and endowment of the individual. The man thinks himself able to know and to do things which once seemed dark and above his grasp. He will do things. "Impossible" is not the word writ in his dictionary. Whatever field of investigation or endeavor he may honor by the dedication of his powers will thenceforth be wider in extent and richer in findings. The man of this self-confidence is not inclined to sympathize with the past. The former generations have not done what they ought. Their richest attainments and highest achievements are not absolutely either high or rich. Even iconoclasm may become the prevailing mood and agent of this spirit. It may attempt to remove the images which humanity has long worshiped. The superstitions which humanity has been content to worship for so long at such shrines, the new soul expels, and searches for better gods to adore.

This self-confidence is usually pretty serious. It conjugates itself in the imperative mood. It has none of the gaiety and frivolity of the world. If a man has been devoting himself to keeping his purple very purple, and his fine linen very fine, and has been wont to fare sumptuously every day, he not unusually is willing to discard his old belongings. In great meters he sings life's psalm, "Life is long, life is earnest." He becomes conscious of responsibility, and of his own responsibility. A change comes to him somewhat akin to that to Donatello of Hawthorne's great romance.

These experiences, too, are characterized by the belief on the part of one having them that they are unique.

He never felt this way before. He had no idea that he ever could feel like this. He had no idea that such an arousing is a part of the life of humanity. Such light as shines upon him never shone before on land or sea. So solitary is he that he is inclined to give no intimation of his experience to even dearest friends. He holds this vision from all eyes; so rich is his discovery, so entrancing his enjoyment, so holy his responsibility, so sacred this communing with himself, that he believes he is enriched as others have not been. His experience is unique. But though he believes this experience is unique and is known to himself alone, others see the change and recognize its significance. They know that this soul is passing through an experience which the best souls have passed through in the process of self-discovery and of self-conquest.

The causes of the beginning of this new life in education and religion are quite as easy to detect as are the evidences of its existence.

Perhaps the most important thing to say about the causes of this awakening is that it may come without special Providence. It may come through the working of the forces which have long been more or less dominant in the individual. Always, too, whatever exterior conditions may become causes, it is the internal powers which transmute these conditions into forces and transform them into controlling influences. In a Christian college the transformation is due to influences which constitute the best part of the course. Enlarging knowledge, deeper reflection, more intimate association with men, represent these influences.

But, both in the college and in the church are powers of three sorts to which this change is not infrequently due: first, a sudden and mighty experience of either joy or sorrow; second, books; third, friendship.

A sudden and mighty experience may give the person passing through it a new life. A father, who came to himself after he had left college, said to me that the birth of his first child transformed him. "I became," he said, "a different man, nobler-minded, and able to bear responsibility and to do things." The death of a parent often teaches the bereft child to see with new eyes, to hear with new ears, to judge with a new-born accuracy, to counsel with a fresher wisdom, to do with a mightier strength. What we call conversion in the Christian sense often is the cause of the intellectual awakening. The heart acts upon the intellect. The man becomes a new creature, not simply in his emotions and volitions, but also in his thoughts.

It is also interesting to trace instances in which books have been the active agent in the awakening of the intellectual or religious life. I must content myself with a single reference. Of President McCosh of Princeton—a preceding lecturer on this historic foundation—it is said: "He was the same reflecting, cautious, self-reliant person on leaving that he had been on entering [college], but with a horizon greatly enlarged, and with an acquired wealth of plain, homely knowledge of human nature. . . . His long intercourse with good books had resulted in a glowing, over-powering desire for fame as a philosopher." [8]

But friendship has also been a cause, possibly more frequent, in the lives of great men, than books. Of Romanes, his biographer says:

> A letter in "Nature" attracted Mr. Darwin's notice, and somewhere about 1874 he invited Mr. Romanes to call on him.
>
> From that time began an unbroken friendship, marked on one side by absolute worship, reverence, and affection, on the other by an almost fatherly kindness and a wonderful interest in the younger man's work and in his career. That first meeting was a real epoch in Mr. Romanes' life. Mr. Darwin met him, as he often used to tell, with outstretched hands, a bright smile, and a "How glad I am that you are so young!"
>
> Perhaps no hero-worship was ever more unselfish, more utterly loyal, or more fully rewarded. As time went on, and intimacy increased, and restraint wore off, Mr. Romanes found that the great master was as much to be admired for his personal character as for his wonderful gifts, and to the youth who never, in the darkest days of utter scepticism, parted with the love for goodness, for beauty of character, this was an overwhelming joy.[9]

This awakened intellectual and religious life has spe-

[8] *The Life of James McCosh,* edited by William Milligan Sloane, p. 36.

[9] *Life and Letters of George John Romanes,* pp. 13-14.

cial relations to certain principles and beliefs which help to constitute this life. The most important of these principles is to be found in the domain of ethics, philosophy, and religion. By means of the chief element of this new life—the element of inquiry—each of these domains, religion, philosophy and ethics, is put under the harrow of grave questioning. Each new soul is pressed with the questions which every new soul that has come into the world, and has come to itself, has put to itself since the beginning. Right, what is it? Wrong, what constitutes it? Why is right right? Why is wrong wrong? Why should I always do the right? Why should I always avoid the wrong? Such are the fundamental questions which the soul asks of itself—and dreadfully real questions are they, too. Upon their answer hang the issues of life and death to the soul. The teaching of the book may help to get the right answer. The talk of a friend may help to get the right answer. But both the teaching and the talk are the materials which the soul must work over satisfactorily to itself. Each soul must find its own answer. In such a struggle no substitution is possible. There can be no vicarious atonement in a battle for an ethical or a religious faith.

Yet this struggle may go from the battlefield of ethics to the broader ground of philosophy and of religion. To the inquiring, struggling soul the problems of philosophy touch the field of religion, and the problems of religion often find their solution in the truths of philosophy. The first questions this soul asks are:

Is there a God? If there is a God, is God a person? And if He be a person, does He know me and can I know Him? If He is a person, what sort of a person is He? If He is good, why does He let the world be so bad? He cannot be omnipotent. If He is omnipotent, He cannot be good, or He would not let the world be so bad. Has God made a law of and for Himself? Where can I turn to find God? Such are some of the questions which the agonizing soul asks of itself, and asks of the world. How many are the men who have found themselves tossing on such a stormy sea of doubt and of questioning! To call the names of some of them is to call the names of those that have come to possess a mighty power and a clear faith. One recalls such an experience in the life of Frederick William Robertson, the great Brighton preacher. One cannot fail to mention the Newmans, too, who, three-quarters of a century ago, were fighting a battle for their faith. In the midst of storm without and within the bosom, these brothers were trying to find an anchorage safe and sure. At last, the one found it (or failed to find it) in the Roman Catholic church, and the other failed to find it, or possibly thought he found it, in what one may call the certainty of life's uncertainties.

Thus, at the beginning of the personal experiences in religion and in education, stands the new birth. Such an identity, or similitude, is significant of the oneness of the being of man. It is also significant of the uniting of religion and of education. In one single center of personal character do the lines, drawn from the circumference, meet.

The process, thus begun, in like relations continues. To the new birth of the soul follows saintliness, or, in the older phrase, sanctification. The vital and vitalizing seed of holiness sprouts, blossoms, and comes to fruitage in character. To the new birth of the mind follows discipline, culture, enrichment, appreciation, power. Time, seizing the single point of newly revealed causation, bears the individual through all experiences into enlarging circles of life. Personal intimacies strengthen the common ties of holiness and of intellectual power. Personal revelations enlarge and give further out-reach to vision. Personal crises teach lessons of holiness to the moral character, and of culture to the reason. The book continues, indeed, to minister, but it must be a book which is, as Milton says, the "precious life-blood of a master-spirit." Life itself becomes an ellipse, drawn from the two centers of religion and of education. This process of culture and of saintliness ends, on one side, in what is called salvation, and, on the other, in what I shall call completion, or wholeness. Perhaps salvation—salvation of spirit, or salvation of intellect—might be used as a crowning word for each. Wholeness, standing for the original meaning of salvation, might be the best. Significant it is that the process in religion and in education, beginning in the new birth, proceeding by culture and sanctification, comes to its zenith and conclusion in salvation, in individual wholeness and completeness.

Society moves toward organization. Society political becomes the government. Society domestic becomes the family. Society religious becomes the church. Society educative becomes the school. The experiences of the individual, of society, become thus incarnated in institutions. The two most important institutions are the family and the civil government. The family begins in the exclusive devotion of a man and woman to each other. Formally recognized in marriage, it is continued in the loyalties of love. It is the pledging of persons to each other. It is, first and foremost, personal. It is religious, becoming more religious as its years increase. If it ceases to be religious, its altars are in grave peril of falling, or at least its holy fires are in danger of burning low. The current tendency toward the destruction of the family has a partial origin in the decline of the religious atmosphere of the home. So long as the constituting members of the family, this husband and wife, this father and mother, maintain the spirit of piety, or the ordinances of religion, so long and so fully does the family maintain its unity of personal blessedness. Be it also said that the family as an educative force is largely personal. The personal influence, feeling, atmosphere, sense of relations of the home, represent its educational value. It cannot easily compete with the school in technical education. But it can, and should, surpass the school in those affections and those personal relations which are to the character what sunlight is to the garden and the wheat field. Likewise, in civil government. If, under the strain of ordinary society, it is difficult to maintain the ascendancy of the persons in the home, how much more difficult under government, complex in relations, embracing tens of millions, or hundreds of millions of citizens, to maintain the power of personality! Civil government becomes institutionalized. It enlarges its functions. It takes on relations economic and social. It is concerned with the administration of many utilities. Its forces enlarge in number and increase in value. Its horsepower, both in physical fact and in poetical metaphor, has magnified unto parabolic proportions. Civil government has become almost a Frankenstein—a monster which creates, devastates, and destroys itself. The direful problems of civil government are created by the lack of great, wise, open-minded, noble-hearted, strong-willed personalities. The problems are the result of the presence of leaders selfish in spirit, narrow in outlook, ignorant of fact, unable to weigh evidence, powerless to understand relations, willing to sacrifice public good to individual pleasure. The need of the civil government is a revival of religion, of personal religion. The need of the civil government is an education which shall purify the heart, make responsive the conscience to the right, strengthen the will unto goodness. Religion through the church, education through the university, should seek to give us such shepherds of the people. The institution of the family, the institution of government, we must have. Conditions determine them. But let them be institutions of great, rich, noble personalities.

As I come to the close of this chapter, I wish to make two suggestions, or to offer two "improvements," as the old sermonizers said:

(1) As experience, education and religion are to be independent, each of the other, yet coöperative, each with the other. Religion may be called the perpendicular in man's life and destiny. It is the relation of man to Ultimate Being which is Divinity. It is to be the object of his aspiration, the end of his supreme achievement. Education is the unfolding of the different powers of the individual and the development of these powers unto their richest, highest, deepest, best. Yet, these two processes, or forces, do coexist, and should colabor. Each is, in a sense, useless without the other. Education is to be religious, and religion is to be educative. They are to be related as the spiral which, as it goes round on itself, goes upward.

(2) This independence of each, and the coöperation of both, are to proceed under supervision and guidance. Without supervision and guidance, the relations ecclesiastic and educational become chaotic. With supervision and guidance, the relations are cosmic. The bishop, the overseer, ecclesiastical and educational, under some form, is to be consecrated. The president, the professor, educational and religious, is to be installed. Each is to co-labor with the other. Plato's philosopher-king is ever to be honored and obeyed. Human experience, as education and religion, is thus made nobler, richer, and more divine.

II

EDUCATION AND RELIGION AS FORM AND CONTENT

In our first lecture, we spoke of education and religion as experience. To-day, I wish to speak of education and religion as form and content.

Education and religion embody a certain likeness of form. Each stands for the human element incarnated in the college and in the church. I now refer, in particular, to three elements of the human side: (1) Both the church and the college use the fact of assemblage of the body of students, or of the congregation of worshipers, who are to be instructed, inspired, and blessed. (2) The human element, also, takes the form as an outward and audible sign of the human voice. The important force, or method, in the propagation is the voice. The preacher speaks his message, the teacher speaks his lesson. It would not be fair to say *vox et praeterea nihil;* better *vox* in the sense of John the Baptist: "Who are you?" "I am a voice." (3) The church has also its sacred books, its historic manuscripts, its creeds, its written dogmas, its elaborated doctrines, the enduring results of the past, of light, of leading, of struggle, of triumph. The college also has its texts, its books, its manuscripts, its libraries, its written and printed statement of teachings offered, accepted, transmuted, transmitted. In their very form, therefore, education and religion are, alike, of impressive similarity.

Historically, too, education and religion are bracketed together. For, in the early medieval period, philosophy became theology, rationalism, ecclesiasticism. In the darkness of that period, it was the lamp of the ecclesiastic, kept trimmed and burning, which helped to dispel the universal night. The schools were cathedral schools; learning belonged to the cloister. It was the transfer of the learning of the monks to the secular college that helped to found the University of Paris, and the succeeding universities of that great age of learning and of teaching. The priest became the professor; the bishop of the diocese, the university chancellor, or vice-chancellor. In nearer historic times, one does not forget that in certain respects the most outstanding college of Oxford is Christ Church, and the largest college of Cambridge is named Trinity. All Souls, Jesus, St. John's, are names of Oxford's colleges. One likes to recall that the Cambridge college most closely associated with our oldest college, and with American higher education, bears the name of Emmanuel. One remembers, with gratitude, that Temple, headmaster of Rugby, became Bishop of London and Archbishop of Canterbury, that the great Stubbs was both a professor of history at Oxford and Bishop of Oxford, and that Westcott was professor at Cambridge and bishop at Durham. Jowett of Balliol was a priest, and T. H. Green and John Richard Green had both taken orders.

An outstanding and recent principal of Glasgow, Story, was an ordained minister of the "kirk," as is George Adam Smith, the beloved principal of Aberdeen. One does not forget that John Henry Newman, the Cardinal, was first a fellow of Oriel. It is a matter of simple academic annals that, for two centuries, every president of Harvard was a clergyman, and that, in order for Theodore Dwight Woolsey (who was professor of Greek) to be elected president of Yale, he was ordained to the ministry. The list, indeed, of great scholars and teachers who have been great churchmen is a quickening one. It is a long one, too, to which the members of an audience like this easily makes many additions. The list begins with Chase for this historic foundation, and it shall not end with the present beloved and efficient President.

But the similarity of form is no more impressive than that of content. By content, I mean the essential and necessary elements and materials of knowledge which constitute religion and education. Be it added that experience and content have a close relation. Experience is both the cause and the result of content. Experience uses knowledge, and, using knowledge, helps to enlarge content. Content is the result of experience. Content, used, results, too, in experience enlarged and made more fruitful.

As content, religion begins with an interpretation of God. The first four words of Genesis, "In the beginning God," is the original and comprehensive text. The verb is, for my present purpose, superfluous. Being is more essential than creation. Creation is the result of being. Theology, in the strict meaning of the word, is the beginning of religion. The doctrine of God is expounded by theologians and philosophers, great and numberless. Absurd it would be for me to attempt to add to their number, or to seek (and in vain) to augment their wisdom. But I do propose to read to you an interpretation which John Henry Newman made, in a book which is devoted both to education and to religion, *The Idea of a University.* The paragraph, too, is a noble piece of literature, as well as a succinct interpretation:

> I mean then by the Supreme Being, one who is simply self-dependent, and the only Being who is such; moreover, that He is without beginning or Eternal, and the only Eternal; that in consequence He has lived a whole eternity by Himself; and hence that He is all-sufficient, sufficient for His own blessedness, and all-blessed, and ever-blessed. Further, I mean a Being, who, having these prerogatives, has the Supreme Good, or rather is the Supreme Good, or has all the attributes of Good in infinite intenseness; all wisdom, all truth, all justice, all love, all holiness, all beautifulness; who is omnipotent, omniscient, omnipresent; ineffably one, absolutely perfect; and such, that what we do not know and cannot even imagine of Him, is far more wonderful than what we do and can. I mean One who is sovereign over His own will and actions, though always according to the eternal Rule of right and wrong, which is Himself. I

> mean, moreover, that He created all things out of nothing, and preserves them every moment, and could destroy them as easily as He made them; and that, in consequence, He is separated from them by an abyss, and is incommunicable in all His attributes. And further, He has stamped upon all things, in the hour of their creation, their respective natures, and has given them their work and mission and their length of days, greater or less, in their appointed place. I mean, too, that he is ever present with His works, one by one, and confronts every thing He has made by His particular and most loving Providence, and manifests Himself to each according to its needs; and has on rational beings imprinted the moral law, and given them power to obey it, imposing on them the duty of worship and service, searching and scanning them through and through with His omniscient eye, and putting before them a present trial and a judgment to come.[1]

Such, in its essence, and as content, is the God of religion. A great definition, isn't it? It may sound a bit mechanical and formal, but it is ever to be borne in the mind, and in the heart, that God belongs to the nature of things. One may believe, with Kant, that His existence cannot be proved. One accepts Him as an assumption, or prolegomenon. Descartes' "I think, therefore I am," one may change into "I am, therefore God is!"

About the doctrine of God are clustered the derived

[1] Pp. 62-63.

doctrines of the form of His existence, as trinity; the doctrine of His relation to man, and of man's relation to Him; the doctrine of His revelation in the Old Testament and the New; the doctrine of eschatology, and the other doctrines which constitute the formal science of religion. The number of such teachings, offered in the schools, is counted by the scores and the hundreds. But the doctrine of God Himself is central, controlling, constructive. It is the center of the great circle of all theological and religious thinking.

By the side of the content of religion, I wish to place the content of education. Before, however, considering the content of education, I wish to say a word regarding two conceptions concerning the higher education, one of which is somewhat new. This more timely conception relates to the idea that the higher education is a pre-picture, or a pre-preparation, or indeed a prophecy, of the subsequent life and work itself. Education is defined as a preparation for life. It is declared that the best preparation for life is life. Life, lived under conditions somewhat akin to those of what is called the larger life, is said to be the best preparation for that larger life. Yet, this preliminary condition is to be made such that the inevitable mistakes will be far less wasteful and disastrous than they would have been upon the subsequent larger and more important arena. Actual experience is desired, and not descriptions of it, or prophecies concerning it. Student activities are declared to be quite as formative as student activity. Doing—the college games and sports, the fraternities, the editorships, the dramatic associations, the singing societies, the chess clubs, and other numberless organizations—are assessed as the most valuable parts of the higher education of the American college. The college is a microcosm. Let it be at once acknowledged that undergraduate activities have value—value in training executive judgment for executive achievement. This value is never to be depreciated. Let it be assessed and accepted at its full worth. Let it also be said that the authorities should not antagonize such movements and their manifestations. Let them seek to guide, and not to abolish. The purpose should be to use the movement and the spirit in such ways as to enrich both the spirit and the movement for the purpose of getting the supreme purpose, the supreme purpose of having youth apply their hearts into wisdom.

A proper conception (as it seems to me) of the higher education of the present is the old conception of getting truth through the content of the curriculum itself. Study your studies. Let the student be a student. This conception represents the essence of the knowledge which constitutes this collegiate body learning and teaching. This content concerns the knowledge of man himself, as seen in history, philosophy, physiology, literature, language, economics, sociology. It concerns the knowledge of nature as set forth under all physical and natural sciences. It concerns the knowledge of God.

My present interpretation, therefore, is that the knowledge of God should be made a part of the course of study of the college and the university. The college of liberal learning should include teaching on the existence of Him in whom we live and move and have our being. Such teaching in the college should not be of the professional type. The college is not a school of theology. The teaching should be of the philosophic type and form. It might well be based upon the philosophy of the Absolute, beginning with Fichte and continuing through Schelling and Hegel. Such teachings concern, of course, God. For, the doctrine of the Absolute is only the doctrine of God writ large. Such interpretations represent the most fundamental, the broadest, the highest questions which the human mind can consider. Examples of such teaching are found in the American college and university. The elder President Dwight of Yale, one of the most outstanding of all American college presidents, preached courses of theological sermons in the college chapel. They were afterwards published in his *System,* a "system" which was studied by many generations of the students of divinity, and also of thoughtful clergymen of the older time. President Franklin Carter gave quickening courses at Williams, on theism. Mark Hopkins' teaching was, both directly and indirectly, related to this comprehensive theme. Such learning and such teaching represent not only good philosophy, but also good theology. At this point, education and religion federated, become united, united in a single comprehensive and formative coöperation.

Education is concerned also, of course, with the

material world. Nature, in many forms, makes its special appeal to the mind of man. It gives a challenge for man's discovery of her secrets, and for his coöperating with her forces. Never in human history was the appeal more appealing, or the challenge more challenging! Of all the several forms of nature's conditions and forces, as named to us—geology, chemistry, physics, biology—the most important for the mutual relations of education and religion is biology. For, the science of biology as botany, and more especially as zoölogy, is now interpreted as having special relationship to theology and religion. The origin of life, the development of life, animal and human, has come to have special relationships to theology. The meaning of the first chapters of Genesis, as interpreting to us the doctrine of God and the doctrine of man, makes a special appeal to the teachings of the biologist touching the origin and the development of life.

The year of 1859 was a *mirabilis annus*. For, in that year, Macaulay died; John Stuart Mill published his *Liberty;* and Charles Darwin published his *Origin of Species*. The doctrine of the *Origin of Species,* and subsequent volumes, were declared to be, by naturalists, like Agassiz, unscientific, and by theologians, like Charles Hodge, atheistic. The scientific criticism has largely passed away. But the theological still abides, and abides in many parts of the new world, in fullness and in violence. Commonwealth after commonwealth, especially of the South, has made or has tried to make, laws prohibiting the teaching, in tax-supported schools, of the theory that man has ascended, or descended, from lower animals. Such laws are based largely on the ground that the evolution hypothesis is atheistic, that, being atheistic, it tends not only to overthrow the church, but also to destroy the state and to disintegrate civil society. The sincerity of those who pass such laws provides no defense for their enactment. Their passage gives evidence that many citizens are still ignorant of what seems to thoughtful men to be a sane interpretation of nature, and of nature's laws and methods.

For, be it said that the theory of development is not concerned with the *origin* of life. That origin is absolutely hidden. Many theories have been adduced. But, as attempts to explain the mystery of beginnings, they seem to be worthless. Every supposition or presupposition is obliged to confess its own nescience. Every prolegomenon is compelled to acknowledge its inability to fathom the infinite mystery. If all nature is derived from a primitive fire mist, as some say, whence then the fire mist? If the electron represents the ultimate, as some intimate, whence the electron? Vain, resultless is the quest. Scientist, metaphysician, theologian, recognize the vanity of the backward search. No Parthian arrow shot by either biologist or philosopher avails.

The present endeavor of the researcher concerns only the method. It is the method of development of life to which we address ourselves. The method does not question what the force which develops nature, human or animal, may be. But it does seek an answer to the problem of the way in which the force, which we call nature, works.

Darwin was not primarily a student of the origin of life. He does, however, in the Preface to the *Origin of Species,* write of life as originally breathed by the Creator into its forms. He was concerned with the origin of species, an origin which assumes and presupposes the supreme fact of life itself. He was concerned with the life in which the Force, whose existence he assumed, worked in the development of species. His theory was, and is, therefore, wholly and absolutely consistent with the theistic principle and assumption. He himself was both surprised and pained with the outburst of certain ecclesiastics against his theory, charging it to be atheistic. In the year 1878, Dr. Pusey preached a sermon against the Darwinian theory. It was published in the "Guardian." Of the sermon, Darwin said himself:

> Dr. Pusey was mistaken in imagining that I wrote the "Origin" with any relation whatever to Theology. . . . Many years ago, when I was collecting facts for the "Origin," my belief in what is called a personal God was as firm as that of Dr. Pusey himself, and as to the eternity of matter I have never troubled myself about such insoluble questions. Dr. Pusey's attack will be as powerless to retard by a day the belief in Evolution, as were the virulent attacks made by divines fifty years ago against Geology, and the still older ones of the Catholic Church against Galileo, for the public is wise enough always to follow Scientific men when

> they agree on any subject; and now there is almost complete unanimity amongst Biologists about Evolution, though there is still considerable difference as to the means, such as how far natural selection has acted, and how far external conditions, or whether there exists some mysterious innate tendency to perfectibility.[2]

Charles Darwin was an agnostic. But, be it firmly said, he was not an atheist. In the year 1874, he wrote to Charles Lyell:

> Many persons seem to make themselves quite easy about immortality and the existence of a personal God, by intuition; and I suppose that I must differ from such persons, for I do not feel any innate conviction on any such points.[3]

In the year 1882, he wrote to Mackintosh, saying:

> Whether the existence of a conscious God can be proved from the existence of the so-called laws of nature (i.e. fixed sequence of events) is a perplexing subject, on which I have often thought, but cannot see my way clearly.[4]

Should one wish for further evidence that Darwin is not concerned with theology, let him refer to the writings of Asa Gray. Asa Gray was called by John Fiske the great scientist of America. The title of one of Gray's books, *Natural Selection Not Inconsistent*

[2] *The Life and Letters of Charles Darwin,* edited by his son, Francis Darwin, Vol. II, p. 412.

[3] *More Letters of Charles Darwin,* edited by his son, Francis Darwin, Vol. II, p. 237.

[4] *Ibid.,* p. 171.

with Natural Theology, gives evidence of his conviction.[5] I may be allowed to add that Asa Gray was a member of an orthodox Congregational Church in Cambridge.

I have dwelt thus long and minutely upon this interpretation of the content of education as found in biology by reason of the timeliness and urgency of the theme. For, the cause of religion is hurt in the house of those who should be its friends and intelligent supporters, and the cause of education is thus limited and made ridiculous by those who should be its defenders. Religion and education, as they meet together in physical science, should be companions, fellow students and neighbors. They are indeed individuals, but they are brothers. They are born of the same parentage. They dwell together under the same infinite firmament. A distinguished scientist and theologian, G. Frederick Wright, professor in an outstanding Ohio college, has said:

> Christian evidence is as really scientific as is that of any of the physical sciences, and that proof in one case is no more certain than in the other. The mysteries underlying the Christian system are no greater than those which underlie every system of knowledge. If Darwinism be a true representation of the manner in which species have come into existence, it only increases the evidence of design.[6]

[5] Asa Gray's *Darwiniana,* p. 87.
[6] *Story of My Life and Work,* p. 200.

The lasting relationship of religion and education is well voiced by verses of Romanes—Romanes, great scientist, great philosopher, who fought his way unto a noble place in science, and unto a firm faith in religion. In a memorial poem on Charles Darwin, he wrote:

> Let Faith and Reason here join hands
> As bride and bridegroom of the mind:
> And only he who understands
> The world that union may unbind;
> For, Lo! the sons of Thought it gains
> In reason as in faith are strong;
> While universal order reigns
> No part can be which proves a wrong,
> But highest reason, highest right,
> And greatest good must still ensure,
> Even though with man should end the light
> Of all that men can deem most pure,
> So let it be that, come what may,
> The very tomb which holds my dust
> Shall bear the message, "Though He slay
> Me, yet in Him shall be my trust." [7]

If the natural sciences form a new part of the college course, having special significance for the church, there is also another group of studies making an appeal to both education and religion. I refer to what might be called the human sciences, or the newer humanities. In this group are included the subjects of economics, government, and sociology. For, economics concerns itself with production; with labor, productive and unproductive; with capital, circulating and fixed; with

[7] *Poems of George John Romanes,* with an introduction by T. Herbert Warren, p. 27.

the laws of its increase; with wages, high or low; with value; with money; with credit; with supply and demand; with trade, national and international; with rates of interest and foreign exchanges; with prices and profits; with debts and taxes—relations which belong to both religion and education. For, the civil government, too, has relations also to religion and education. Under this government, the church has a certain separate existence, and under this government, the college holds its property and offers its education. Sociology, moreover, concerns man both as a citizen of society and as a child of God. It is related to men in groups. It studies the origin, the history, the progress of society, the laws governing human intercourse, in order that it may deduce a scientific basis for the conscious control of man, that through progress, both for the race and for the individual, noblest perfection may be the ultimate result. Likewise, the church concerns itself with men in groups. It gathers individuals together in public worship, in Sunday schools, in its devotional and teaching meetings of the week day, and in its assemblies of various other sorts. Through and upon these groups the church works. It studies the different classes out of which the church body is created, and it endeavors by sermon, by teaching, by precept, and by example, to interpret God—to lift man out of the influence of the materialism which is temporal, and upward unto the things of the spirit which are eternal.

To two other contents I wish to refer. They touch both education and religion. The first is literature.

Literature is the finest fruitage of the tree of knowledge. It incarnates and voices the highest thinking, the deepest feeling, the supreme struggle of every people. On the topmost branch of this tree of life, open alike to the calm sunshine of reflection and stirred by the storms of emotion, hangs that form of literature called the poem. I would that literature, in the form of poetry or the essay, or reflective history, might be made to have a larger place in the teaching of the literary college and of the professional school of theology. To the student of liberal learning, literature gives intellectual quickening and enrichment, and to the professional student, it bears priceless treasures. It is also to be remembered that, in the sermon of the preacher, literature represents a spring of refreshing, outflowing, grateful to the taste, and nourishing to the spiritual strength of an appreciative and responsive congregation. It is indeed a cause of gratitude that our English literature bears precious treasures, in its content, to both education and religion. It is both educative and Christianizing, and, for several reasons, fundamental and timely. It is the embodiment of the noblest history of a great people. It forms one of the finest illustrations of the law of causality. It embraces forces and conditions, both subjective and objective, working together under a vast variety of forms to effect great human results. It is, with the three exceptions of the Greek, the French, and the Hebrew, the longest in point of time, the richest in content, the most diverse in literary movement. It is, above all other literatures, the most ethical in its teachings and the most Christian in its impressiveness. It lacks the aesthetic principles and forms of some Romantic literatures. It gives constant heed to the moral reason of things. The wealth of this ethical content is of immeasurable worth. The content is vitally associated with its creators. The amount of its wealth is hardly less impressive than is the variety of its vast resources. No other literature offers diversities so extreme. Shakespeare, the universal interpreter, "the experiencing" mind, the man of the world, is followed by Milton, the moralist in prose, the theologian in verse, the Puritan pamphleteer, striking at the evils of his own age, the poet whose name is linked with that of Virgil and of Dante. Addison, the union of morality, of religion, of literature, and of eloquence, follows Milton, being at once grave and humorous, elevated and commonplace, whose writing beats in harmonious music and is woven of the strand of noble conduct. He, in turn, is succeeded by Swift, both vulgar and gifted, witty and brusque, unhappy, scornful, proud, impatient, skeptical, energetic, hated and hating, but of a power which puts him with the immortals. In the fast-coming generations Wordsworth appears, writing verses of highest inspiration (and also lines of common doggerel), the philosopher and the ethical interpreter in poetry. Shelley and Keats emerge as singers of romance, and Tennyson as the recorder of the Middle Age chivalry and mystery, and chanting, like the Greek tragedians, to the despairing heart of man. Browning comes forth as the virile optimist in the prose song, the shadow of a great rock in a weary land, and, it may be added, a wall of defense for the morally tempted. The novelists, too, in the later decades become regnant. Walter Scott, the bringer-back of the later chivalry; Dickens, the painter of the common life of the common people; and Thackeray, the interpreter of the common life of a higher human zone. The essayists, too, come forth, a mighty army—Newman, the mystic, the unsurpassed master of a limpid style, the singer of prose music; Macaulay, the orator in history and essay, as well as in the House of Commons, martial, majestic, the incarnation of English political liberalism; John Stuart Mill, metaphysician, economist, logician, rationalist, an intellect devoted to highest purposes; Carlyle, a John the Baptist, proclaiming his own coming indeed, a combination of great-mindedness and of shattered nerves, to whom emotions had the value of inductions, a poet without rhyme—and sometimes without reason—yet a voice far-reaching in its shrill cries, an interpreter whose lessons are to abide, an inspiring and affirming force—these, and more also, are the types, constant or sporadic, of literature and of its creators, which England offers to the student seeking the best education for himself. Time and space would fail one to tell of Bacon, the philosopher of nature; of Edmund Burke, the philosopher in statesmanship; of Defoe, of Richardson, of Fielding, of Goldsmith, of Jane Austen, of Samuel Johnson, and of the later essayists and poets and historians who have wrought well, coming out of a long and rich and diverse past, to us of the present age.

To one other great content of both education and religion, I must be allowed to refer. It is philosophy. Under philosophy I include psychology, metaphysics, epistemology. But philosophy is less a subject than an angle of vision. It is less a subject than a union of all subjects, less knowledge than wisdom, less wisdom than a love of wisdom. It is an aspiration, an inspiration, a questioning. With the great Garman, almost adopting his words, I may say that the fundamental truths underlying are idealism, personality, and sovereignty. These truths are far more important, far more essential, far more necessary, than any truths found in Freudism or behaviorism. As the inspiring Amherst teacher says:

> The conception of the universe, material as truly as moral, as dependent on God for its continued existence from moment to moment, as truly as the rainbow on the continued shining of the sun. Philosophy takes literally Christ's words, that not a sparrow falls to the ground "without your Father." So also the words of the Apostle Paul: "For in Him we live, and move, and have our being."
>
> . . . The conception of Personality is the ultimate fact of the universe. From which it follows that all nature as truly as all human history has not merely a scientific, but also an ethical and a religious, import, and is progressing towards the realization of divine ideals. This is the founda-

> tion for all true optimism. Philosophy deals with practical pantheism by tracing it to its sources. . . .[8]
>
> The great doctrine of Sovereignty is the third of the jewels that crystallize out of philosophical discussions. . . . It is the utlimate principle of all personal relationship, not merely between God and man, but quite as much between man and his fellows. Philosophy shows that human government and divine government stand or fall together. . . . There is no government where there are no sanctions to the law, for then laws become mere advice. When men realize this, the fact of an atonement is their only hope for mercy.[9]

Thus philosophy and theology are made to belong together in education and religion, which also belong together.

Such are some of the primary and elemental contents which constitute education and religion as they coexist in their relationship to each other. They seem to me to be first in importance and first in constructiveness. They are the truths which underlie derived knowledges in every department of thought. Their value, as seen in different subjects, of course differs, but, in some degree of worth, they help to constitute these two great fields, or movements, of thought and endeavor. To these themes—the doctrine of God, the natural sciences, the newer humanities, literature, and

[8] *Letters, Lectures and Addresses of Charles Edward Garman:* A Memorial Volume, prepared by Eliza Miner Garman, p. 420.

[9] *Ibid.,* p. 423.

philosophy—I would, for both education and religion, give complete devotion and loyalty.

In contrast with these, the great thoroughfares of education and religion, I venture to indicate that there are certain alleys or bypaths, that might be called private ways, and therefore should be marked "dangerous." They might be called *isms*. One *ism* of religion is that all creeds are equally good, if one really believes them. The corresponding *ism* of education is, all studies are equally valuable, if one only pursues them equally hard. A second *ism* of religion is that children should not be taught religion, but left to decide their own faith on reaching mature years. The corresponding *ism* of education is that children should be left to themselves, to educate themselves as they see fit. A third *ism* of religion is that all beliefs are vain, and are as nothing, that the priest, or the minister, is the all-in-all in religion. The corresponding *ism* of education is that what you study is nothing, that the man who teaches you is the only concern. A fourth *ism* of religion is that most people cannot be religious, and therefore no attempt should be made to evangelize them. The corresponding *ism* of education is that most people cannot be educated, and therefore no endeavor should be made to teach them. A fifth *ism* of religion is that all churches are bad—therefore avoid them. The corresponding *ism* of education is that all colleges are poor—therefore keep out of them. A sixth *ism* of religion is, Be *your* best, write your own creed, make your own God. The corresponding *ism* of education is, Be your own teacher, choose your own books, learn your own lessons, educate yourself. Such are a few of the many sidepaths which lead off of the main historic ways of both education and of religion.

The barest statement of such *isms* proves their own refutation. The general answer to them each and all is that they fail to bear evidence of reality, intellectual and spiritual. Every course of study must possess, as a central and formative force, the element of reality. This element interprets things as they are. It gives a sense of proportion. It presents truths truthfully. It has a sense of cubical relationships, but it is never cubist. It has a sense of harmony, but it is not jazz. Spiritual reality must underlie, penetrate, and canopy-over the content of both religion and education.

As I close, one remark emerges. This interpretation makes plain that the content of religion, as knowledge, vastly enlarges. It is also made equally plain that the content of education, as knowledge, vastly enlarges. No prophetic vision is required to declare that the enlargement is still to continue, and to continue apparently for unnumbered ages, and unto relationships limitless. Meantime, the capacity and competency of the human mind and heart, conscience, and will have not enlarged in equivalent proportions. The person is obliged to labor as an atom in this enlarging firmament. His resulting duty, his only duty perhaps, is to select out of the infinite field a microscopic section which he may know, cultivate, and bring to fruitage. The consequent lesson, which one is at once to learn and to practice, is the lesson of gratitude, of humility, and of exultation. It is the lesson of Pascal: man is only an atom. But he is an atom which thinks, reasons, chooses —an atom which has relationships to the Infinite, to the Eternal, to Omniscience itself. To him, therefore, both education and religion in their common form and content make an appeal immediate and lasting.

III

EDUCATION AND RELIGION IN RELATION TO THE REASON AND OTHER FACULTIES OF MAN

THE first lecture was concerned with education and religion as experience; the second with education and religion as form and content. In the present lecture, I wish to consider education and religion as appealing to the reason and other faculties of man.

For, first and foremost, education does address itself to the human reason. By reason, I mean the whole intellectual faculty and function of man. I mean understanding; I mean the knowing, the thinking, the logical faculty. In it I include the pure and the practical, the inductive and deductive, the logical and the discursive, the speculative, the theoretical, and the intuitive elements of reason.

To such a faculty, education addresses itself. As to the eye light comes, and the union of light and of the eye brings objects into its seeing; as to the ear come certain vibrations of the air, and the union of these vibrations with the ear gives what are called sounds; as to the touch comes hardness of objects, and as from the union follows a sensation—so an exterior sensation comes to the reason. From the union is derived knowledge or truth, of the exterior world, or a knowledge of truth. Thus, fact added to fact, of man, of man's history, man's government, man's affiliations, man's entire relationship, creates man's knowledge. This whole process—begun in earliest youth, conducted through the early and the late adolescent period, pushed forward into the third decade of life, bearing knowledge of all sorts, supervised by teachers, systematized, adjusted, part to part, progressive, from the simple to the complex, from the complex to the more complex, quickened by purpose, guided by wisdom, enforced by example, inspired by companionship—represents the higher education. It stands for the crowning of the sovereignty of the human reason. *Veritas,* a word inscribed across three open books, forming the shield of the oldest American college, represents the authority of the reason. It is the force and the agent, knowing and declaring the truth. *Lux et Veritas* inscribed on the shield of the third oldest college, and other colleges, too, stands likewise for the authority, the cause, the result, of the human reason.

There is the greater cause for emphasizing this truth of the appeal which the higher education makes to the reason, because of the voices in the air declaring that what some of us would hold to be secondary values of education are indeed primary. It is said that the higher education is not valuable in its rational relations. It is declared that many activities are more important than the single activity. It is said that the sports and the games, the clubs, fraternities, and societies provide an education more formative than the classroom. It is said, jocosely, that "your studies should not be allowed to interfere with your college life." Let us recognize the worth of all these facts and forces. Let all authorities seek to use these conditions and forces for securing the highest purposes. But ever let it be remembered that the studium is more important than the stadium. To apply one's heart unto wisdom is chief. Wisdom is the principal thing; therefore, "with all thy getting, get understanding." Understanding is primary, and the way of getting understanding is through the great teacher, the great book, the great theme, the great thinking.

Likewise, reason is the supreme force of man in relation to religion. At this point, one strikes into a theological highway whence radiate many bypaths, and into which, also, many well-traveled ways come. Care must therefore be taken not to be misled.

I therefore venture to make certain propositions regarding the relation of reason to religion.

(1) Religion comes unto man through the reason, and through other faculties also. Religion cannot be unrational. Much less, it cannot be anti-rational. It may be, it is, super-rational in certain relations. For, it deals with truths which the reason is unable to weigh as it weighs scientific truths. Yet, the evidence for accepting these truths is stronger than the evidence for rejecting them. The reason never forces itself to say that religion is to be accepted more completely as the evidence for it is more completely unrational, or anti-rational. The heights of religion are higher than the

flights of reason. But the pathways of religion, so far as they do mount up, go in the direction of the understanding.

(2) The truths of religion are based on evidence. This evidence is primarily addressed to the reason. Its items are indeed to be analyzed. Its parts are to be assessed at a just value. Objections are to be weighed. The whole synthesis is a body of truth for the acceptance of the reason, for the guidance of the conscience, and for the inclusion in formal statement, either as *obiter dicta* or as dogmatic symbols.

(3) Religion is to respect the laws of reason, and reason is to respect the faiths and the creeds of religion. Reason cannot jump out of its cranium! It cannot commit suicide! If it hear a voice from the heavens, like Paul, it also, like Paul, is to inquire whose is that voice. It must distinguish between the flashes from the nether pits and the illumination of the heavenly vision. It is often called to judge between some other gospel, which may captivate the unthinking, and the gospel of the Son of God, addressed to the sons of rational men. It is to discriminate. Revelation and reason have a similar purpose and, therefore, may use a not dissimilar method. Both coöperate.

(4) Reason enjoys the birthright of freedom. It is its own *ipse dixit.* Its authority, its sovereignty, are its own. It is its own legislative, judicial, and executive power. Properly interpreted, it reads its own Bible for its guidance, acknowledges itself as its own authority for making decrees, which indeed may be fallible, and

accepts the determination of its own councils which it does create under its own seal.

Such seem to me to be the quartette of principles which religion uses in its appeal to the reason of man, which the reason of man uses in its relationship to religion. They are, to recapitulate: (1) Religion comes unto man through the reason; (2) the truths of religion are based on evidence; (3) religion is to respect the laws of reason, and reason is to respect the faiths and the creeds of religion; (4) reason has the birthright of freedom. These propositions belong primarily to the church which is called Protestant.

The opinion is common that the Roman Catholic church holds doctrines wholly different. It has, however, been said that "We are as much bound to submit our *intellect* to God as we are bound to submit our *will* to Him." [1] What is it indeed "to submit our intellect to God?" Is it not to affirm that it is the more reasonable to submit the intellect to God than to be arrogant, selfish, self-centered, self-ruling, autocratic? Is it any other than to say it is more rational to be rational than to be unrational? Reason still rules in its methods and unto its conclusions negative and positive. A most constructive part of the reason, moreover, is the conscience. That scholar of the church, John Henry Newman, says of the conscience:

> Conscience is the aboriginal Vicar of Christ, a prophet in its informations, a monarch in its peremptoriness, a priest in its blessings and

[1] *Catholic Belief*, by Very Rev. J. Faa di Bruno, p. 194.

> anathemas, and, even though the eternal priesthood throughout the Church could cease to be, in it the sacerdotal principle would remain and would have a sway. . . . Did the Pope speak against conscience in the true sense of the word, he would commit a suicidal act. He would be cutting the ground from under his feet. His very mission is to proclaim the moral law, and to protect and strengthen that "Light which enlighteneth every man that cometh into the world." On the law of conscience and its sacredness are founded both his authority in theory and his power in fact . . . it is by the universal sense of right and wrong, the consciousness of transgression, the pangs of guilt, and the dread of retribution, as first principles deeply lodged in the hearts of men, it is thus and only thus, that he has gained his footing in the world and achieved his success.[2]

Perhaps I have drawn too heavily upon your attention in interpreting the extent to which both education and religion appeal to the reason. More than enough has been said to make plain that both these primary forces address themselves to the reason of man.

Let us, therefore, at once pass on to indicate a similitude of appeal to another great faculty, the heart of man. It is important that the heart of man should be included in the relation which religion and education bear. For, the reason is not the single object of appeal.

[2] *The Mystery of Newman,* by Henri Bremond, translated by H. C. Corrance, p. 336.

A type of education and of religion which should make an appeal to the reason alone would be narrow indeed. It would lack richness and fullness. It would be in danger, if it were profound, of being bare and barren, and, if it were effective for practical purposes, of being superficial. Such an appeal would certainly be unhumane, unhumanistic, and unhuman.

Therefore, I appeal for an education and a religion which, together, address themselves to the feelings of man. Students like ourselves are in peril of depreciating the worth of the feelings in the higher education. I would not say that we have overemphasized intellect, but we have underemphasized emotion. Even John Stuart Mill has left precious testimony upon this primary worth and relationship:

> Sentiments, which by comparison at least may be called elevated, are the current coin of human intercourse, both in books and in private life; and though often evaporating in profession, are yet kept alive in the nation at large by constant exercise, and stimulated by sympathy, so as to form a living and active part of the existence of great numbers of persons, and to be recognized and understood by all. Neither could I then appreciate the general culture of the understanding, which results from the habitual exercise of the feelings, and is thus carried down into the most uneducated classes of several countries on the Continent, in a degree not equalled in England among the so-called educated, except where an unusual tenderness of conscience leads to a habitual exer-

cise of the intellect on questions of right and wrong.[8]

The realm of the feelings is, indeed, ruled over by both education and religion. In religion, feeling is chiefly of two kinds: (1) the emotion of love—of love to God. This feeling is, of course, born of the Being who is interpreted as Love. This feeling is even more structural and comprehensive than is the feeling of worship of One who is Omniscient, than is the feeling of adoration of One who is Omnipresent and Omnipotent. (2) The second feeling is the feeling of dependence. You recall that Schleiermacher, a teacher as devout as Kant, as idealistic as Fichte, makes religion to consist in the feeling of dependence. The element of feeling, be it added, does not in religion exist alone. For, the heart acts on the understanding, and the understanding on the heart. The two are coöperative. Remember Pascal's words:

> We know the truth, not only by the reason, but also by the heart; it is by the heart that we know first principles, and it is in vain that reasoning, which has no part in it, tries to combat them. . . . It is on this knowledge of the heart and instinct that reason must support herself, and on this she founds her whole procedure. . . . Principles are felt, propositions are proved; and all with certainty, although in different ways. And it is as ridiculous for the reason to demand of the heart proofs of its first principles, in order to be willing

[8] *Autobiography,* p. 59.

> to consent to them, as it would be for the heart to demand of the reason a feeling of all the propositions that it demonstrates in order to be willing to receive them.[4]

Likewise, the feelings have their function in education. These feelings in relation to education are, as in the case of religion, summarized in the feeling of love. This feeling of love relates largely to a teacher. In education, one great need is the need of teachers for whom students do feel the emotion of love. Few, altogether too few, are the teachers who quicken this emotion in their students. At the present moment, I shall name three, and three only. The first is Sumner of Yale. William Graham Sumner was professor at Yale for thirty-seven years, beginning in 1872 and ending in 1909. "The display of affection and love which moved Sumner more probably than any other came at the close of his career."[5] The description of the conferring upon him of the degree of doctor of laws gives a basis for judging of the reality and the fullness of the love in which he was held:

> The hall was filled with two generations of men whom he had taught and inspired. One after another the candidates were called up and each was greeted with scattering applause. Sumner was last on the list, and when his name was announced there was a terrific outburst. Fathers and sons stood up together, clapping their

[4] *The Thoughts, Letters, and Opuscules of Blaise Pascal,* translated from the French by O. W. Wight, pp. 248-249.

[5] *William Graham Sumner,* by Harris E. Starr, p. 546.

hands, shouting at the top of their voices, and even waving their hats. Sumner arose and, somewhat confused and unsteady on his feet, moved to the center of the stage where he stood bowed over a little, while the hurricane of cheers continued. It was evident that he was embarrassed and did not know what to do; his face grew red, and he pulled nervously at his mortarboard; but still the racket kept up. Suddenly the hall was as still as a church, and Professor William Lyon Phelps, who was introducing the candidates, began to speak: "The history of Professor Sumner's life," he said, "during the last thirty-seven years is in large measure the history of Yale. Always a radical"—at the word "radical" Sumner straightened his shoulders like a shot, just as a war horse throws up his head at the sound of a distant bugle. The audience roared again, the movement was so characteristic of the man, and it was several minutes before Professor Phelps could go on. "Always a radical in educational policies," he finally continued, "head of the liberal element in the faculty, he has seen Yale change from a conservative to a progressive institution. If victory is sweet to those who fight, his heart must be warm." At this statement, Sumner pulled his nose with a nervous jerk, and for a third time the audience shouted, appreciating with keen relish that Sumner there on the stage, sniffing at eulogies, was the same man he had always been, the very embodiment of primeval truthfulness and ruggedness. "Professor Sumner has combined to an extraordinary degree the

> patience of the scholarly investigator with the fiery zeal of those who love truth. Like all great teachers and real leaders of men, he is intensely dogmatic; but his dogmas are not the result of narrowness or prejudice; they come from prolonged study and profound thought. His intellect has broadened, his heart has mellowed, as he has descended into the vale of years. He has set all of us a great example—in having a hospitable mind; a mind not afraid of intellectual consequences, open to every new idea, and ready to give it glad welcome. . . . He possesses the love, respect and veneration of his former pupils; we do not know 'what social classes owe to each other,' but we do know that many classes at Yale owe Professor Sumner more than can be compassed within the limits of language."[6]

The second of the great college teachers who have been greatly loved is Garman of Amherst—Charles Edward Garman, who taught philosophy for more than twenty-five years. Of Garman it is said: "It was because there was first of all this great personality, with a genuine interest in every student, that Professor Garman has achieved the immortality which Plato tells us every great soul craves, the living on in ideals, aspirations, and enthusiasms that it has begotten in other souls."[7] Garman held, and still holds in memory, his

[6] *Ibid.*, pp. 546-548.

[7] *Letters, Lectures and Addresses of Charles Edward Garman*, prepared by Eliza Miner Garman, p. 47.

students by the power of a great love for them—a love both of the heart and of the will.

Of another teacher, Palmer of Harvard, it is ever to be said that he quickened and held the love of students. No less than fifteen thousand has he numbered in his long service at our oldest college. Of him, his colleague, Royce, once said:

"I deeply regret that I was not in the ordinary sense his pupil. You who have been his pupils know that herein I have lost much. But this I know, that we can none of us ever lose him or his influence so long as we continue either to reflect or to love." [8]

After the death of Royce, Palmer wrote of him, saying, "Happy the University that had for a long time so vitalizing a presence!" [9] The simple eulogy one may transfer to Palmer himself, and in the transferring make the interpretation wider. Happy the student who has, as a teacher and as a friend, one so wise, so quickening, and so gifted as is George Herbert Palmer.

An illustration of the emotional relation of both education and religion, as seen in the college and the church, is found in two aspects of each of these institutions. The primary aspect of each deserves the word invisible. In annals historical and ecclesiastical we read of the contrast between the church visible and the church invisible. The church visible we see in institutions, in historic architecture, in mighty goings-forth of

[8] "In Honor of Professor Palmer," by Josiah Royce, *The Harvard Graduates' Magazine,* Vol. XIX, 1911, No. 76, p. 578.

[9] "Josiah Royce," by George Herbert Palmer, *ibid.,* Vol. XXV, 1916, No. 98, p. 170.

missionary and evangelistic zeal. We hear its voices in *Te Deums, Glorias,* and *Magnificats,* in the discourses of the Chrysostoms and the Savonarolas. There is a church invisible. Throughout all the ages, it is found in the glorious company of the apostles whose works remain unrecorded, in the testimony of the martyrs whose voices were stilled by sword or smothered in flame, in the witnessing of scholars, reading faded manuscripts in dim, sepulchral lights, in the petitions of saints, praying at historic altars, in the patience of prophets, teaching in desert monasteries, or proclaiming God's truth in basilica and cathedral. This, too, represents the church, and the church invisible.

No less significant is the likeness or the difference between the college visible and the college invisible. Open your eyes, and you see the college visible, in buildings historic, devoted to life and to learning, in chapel and library, and hall of science—a hall of science bearing the name of a beloved apostle of piety—a lover of scholarship, a friend of scholars. Open your ears, and you hear it, this college visible, audible in the shouts of students all at play. But there is also a college quite as real, the college invisible. The college of midnight vigils, of unspoken longings, of quiet sacrifices, buried deep in cloistered wall, the college of memories, precious as sacramental wine to dying lips, the college of companionships as immortal as life, the college of youth which knows no age, the college of teachers beloved as is parents' love, the college of visions which await realization beyond the stars—that is the college invisible which builds itself hard by the college visible. It also builds itself hard by the church invisible. Equally real, equally human, equally heavenly, each is let down from the skies for the edification of man through the oracles of God, each having its own great cloud of witnesses, and the two assemblages seeming as one.

Education and religion, likewise, make a common appeal to the aesthetic sense, as well as to the reason and to the heart. Of all the faculties of man, the aesthetic is the most difficult to define. I shall make no attempt. But, accepting diverse definitions, one easily discovers the new identities of the appeal which the two great forces of education and religion make to the aesthetic faculty. If one, with Plato, accept beauty as standing for symmetry, it is clear that religion gives such a conception in its demand for the creation of the fitness of things, and in the supremacy of the Idea or the Ideal. Education, also, calls upon the same faculty in its requirement that nothing shall be excessive and nothing shall be lacking. If one, with Hegel, reason that the beautiful is the absolute in sensuous existence, or experience, he finds that religion recognizes the Absolute as a form or definition of his God, and he also finds that education reaches out toward such a stage in its training of the human soul in its progress toward the infinite. If one accept the basis of the beautiful as found in *truth,* it is not difficult to believe that religion, founding itself upon truth, does possess attributes of the beautiful. It is also likewise natural to believe that education, using knowledge of the truth as its tool and instrument, does take on the qualities of the beautiful. If one assent to the principle that the beautiful is essentially related to repose and to moderation, it is no remote inference to affirm that religion, abiding in the very peace of God, is also the exponent of the beautiful. It is likewise clear that education, dealing with problems of the eternal and universal spirit, is endowed with the great elements of the beautiful. If it is said, as it is said, that the idea of beauty purifies and exalts the human soul, it is also evident that education and religion are akin in this force. For, both are the forces most purifying and exalting to man. If it is said, further, that the consummation of the beautiful is to be found in a world beyond time and space, it is further to be declared, and with a spirit of exultation and of exaltation, that both education and religion seek to fit the soul of man for the eternal enjoyment of God, and that it seeks to train the character for a life beyond life. To the beautiful, therefore, however interpreted, education and religion make a like appeal. In the same realm, they are fellow-citizens, the saint becoming the scholar, and the scholar the saint.

If one were to seek for illustrations of education and religion as meeting in the field of the beautiful, his quest would meet with glorious and full rewards. The cathedrals of France, of Italy, built for the worship of God, are the triumphs of the great architects, of Michelangelo and of his pupils. The madonnas of

Raphael, of Murillo, of Andrea del Sarto, represent the skill of the learned and the devotions of the saints. Great art, in painting, in sculpture, in architecture, is ever religious. Religion expresses itself in great art. If one were to seek for a single example of the union of education and of religion in the beautiful and the sublime, would he not turn to the Vatican and to its Sistine Chapel, where, four centuries ago, Michelangelo placed the history of man—of man as the child of God and as the child of human destiny? The Sistine Chapel is Dante's "divine comedy" put into fadeless color, in enduring space. It is the unfolding of the faith and education of man from his creation unto the consummation of all things.

Moreover, it is to be affirmed that both education and religion make an appeal to the moral faculty of man, as well as to the aesthetic, the emotional, and the rational. Conscience is a regent in human character, and some would say, the sole regent. For, the moral faculty stands for the sense of moral obligation. Moral obligation is only the word duty writ double. It is said that Kant's ethics has lost its historic leadership, but the categorical imperative does still remain. It stands for the "Thou shalt," and "Thou shalt not," of the divine command. This is the very opposite of the teaching of the eighteenth century, a teaching which Pope aptly embodied in the phrases:

> Reason's whole pleasure, all its joys of sense,
> Lie in the words, wealth, peace, and competence.

It demands, and incites unto, absolute obedience. It

does not threaten. It does not insinuate reward. It holds out no prize. It closes no door to purgatory. It opens no pearly gate. Whether your conception of duty be inductive or deductive, or whether it be founded on sympathy, as Adam Smith said it was founded, or on the principle of universal happiness, as has argued Paley, is not our present concern. The present concern is that the concept of moral obligation is to be observed, of duty to be heeded. It is a concept made a duty which education disciplines, and which religion enforces.

This conception, most commanding and compelling, has special meaning for college men. For them, education and religion give a beauty and an emphasis which no other teaching offers. The element of duty, instructed by education and quickened by religion, has, for college men, its most outstanding illustration in the services of the student and the graduate in war. As a college president, I have seen college students go forth to two wars, the Spanish, and the one rightly called the Great War. I have seen the boys go forth, and I have not seen them come back. I read the names of some of them on memorial tablets in college chapels. Not alone, too, in American universities are their names inscribed. In Oxford and Cambridge, in Glasgow and Edinburgh, in the University of Paris, the lists are longer, far longer. Let us also acknowledge that Berlin and Leipzig and Heidelberg gave themselves for what their sons called "duty to Fatherland." Each duty calls to each. Duty inspired by religion, duty taught by education, are the summons which they heard and obeyed. As sang Rupert Brooke:

Blow out, you bugles, over the rich Dead!
 There's none of these so lonely and poor of old,
 But, dying, has made us rarer gifts than gold.
These laid the world away; poured out the red
Sweet wine of youth; gave up the years to be
 Of work and joy, and that unhoped serene,
 That men call age; and those who would have been,
Their sons, they gave, their immortality.

Blow, bugles, blow! They brought us for our dearth,
 Holiness, lacked so long, and Love, and Pain.
Honour has come back, as a king, to earth,
 And paid his subjects with a royal wage;
And Nobleness walks in our ways again;
 And we have come into our heritage.[10]

Kipling also sings:

He scarce had need to doff his pride or slough the dross of Earth—
E'en as he trod that day to God so walked he from his birth,
In simpleness and gentleness and honour and clean mirth.
So cup to lip in fellowship they gave him welcome high,
And made him place at the banquet board—the Strong Men ranged thereby,
Who had done his work and held his peace and had no fear to die.[11]

But, in the daily round, duty is no less commanding, and the common task no less imperative. Let us bring to its doing the exultation of the warrior and the vision of the prophet. Thank God, that, in a college like

[10] "The Dead"
[11] Quoted in *Letters of Gilbert Little Stark.*

this, standing for education and for religion, of the past and of the present and of the future, the call of duty is disciplined, enlarged, strengthened, and is obeyed.

IV

EDUCATION AND RELIGION AS DEVELOPING FORCES AND AS CONSUMMATION

WE now come to the fourth, and last, lecture in our course. Having considered education and religion as experience, as having a certain form and content, and as making an appeal to the reason and other faculties of man, I now venture to ask you to think of these two great powers, or conditions, both as forces, and also as representing consummation.

For, education and religion may be interpreted as forces. They are dynamic. Primarily, these forces are human and personal. They may use, but they are not, the powers of nature, organic or inorganic. To the human personality they appeal, and from the human personality they are projected. As I have already intimated, they are forces taking on forms intellectual, ethical, emotional, of the will, of the sense of beauty, of the conscience. Education and religion constitute, and are constituted by, forces. They are not statical. They are gifted with movement. As matter seems to be dynamic, so are they. Expressing themselves in institutions—the church, the college, the family—they still are quick with life. As forces, they occupy angles of vision, of the universe and of eternity. They intimate that man is a citizen of a universe of infinite distances and destinies, of infinite relations in time, as well as in space. Education and religion are alike in their sights and insights, in their reach, in their grasp, in their opportunities, in their hopes, in their loyalties, and in their infinite visions. As the earth and all its celestial companions are moving through space apparently endless, so education and religion are likewise going forth in an infinite universe through God's eternal time.

Such forcefulness on the part of education and religion is made the more necessary by reason of the powers of darkness of the present age. I would not be a Cassandra. But it is clear that the five institutions of society—the civil government, the church, the school, the family, and property—are beset by the powers of evil. Government tends to become either a monarchy, dictatorship, or a loosely organized or ineffectively administered democracy. The institution of property, the result of a long and hard historic struggle, suffers the disintegration of the communist. The family, through excessive individualism and the changes of industrial organization, tends toward disintegration. Therefore, to the forces of education and of religion should be added, in the greatest possible degree, inspiration, unity, compactness, directness. Education should become more religious without becoming less educative. Religion should be made more educative without becoming less religious or Christian. In the last decades, the scientific forces have taken on a forcefulness which might deserve the epithet infinite. Think of what the names of Roentgen, Brush, Rutherford, Einstein, represent! Perhaps the increase of forces, suggested by such names, cannot be, in the nature of things, applied to education and religion. But these very names are a call for the educationist and for the Christian to use every effort of mind and of will, of heart and of conscience, of condition and of personality, unto vast enlargements and enrichments.

This interpretation of the fact of forces prepares the way for a brief presentation of the consummations which await.

The first fruit of the tree of education and of religion is what I shall call a synthesis of the conditions, forces, methods, causes, and results which constitute the whole character of the individual. In the constitution of the character of the individual, the three steps, or forms, which Hegel intimates as belonging to philosophy, obtain. They are thesis, antithesis, and synthesis. A belief is met by a disbelief, and the two are united in a belief more comprehensive. A truth is set opposite a truth and the pair are joined in a trinity. William James writes of four forms of saintliness—devoutness, purity, chastity, asceticism. Devoutness may become fanaticism, purity abnormality, chastity nonresistance, asceticism unworldly remoteness and personal destruction. But, on the other and better side, devoutness may become worship, sane and beautiful; purity, forthputting energy and zeal; chastity, service; and asceticism, self-sacrifice for the betterment of all.

Each doctrine of religion faces, like Janus, two ways. It may be solidified into a human dogma or interpretation. It may be sublimated into airy Hegelian abstractions. Each doctrine, however, is to be interpreted as a divine truth, understood by and for the human reason. Each fact, or principle, of education is likewise double-faced. It may be stated as a theory, remote, having relationship only to empty space and empty time. It also may be interpreted as a daily round and a common task. It is to be accepted as a principle, born of both philosophy and psychology, and used for the discipline and the making of the modern mind. Comte commends, as a step in human progress, analysis of phenomena. It is a worthy commendation. He also commends, as a higher stage, synthesis, and the higher commendation is even more worthy. Dichotomy is good and necessary. Trichotomy is also good and necessary. But, quite as necessary, and better, is wholeness which unites the twos and the threes. Let us have individuality. Let us also have conformity. Let us also have unity. Let there be orthodoxy. Let there also be heterodoxy and heresy. Let us have the logical values of life, also the ethical, and also the aesthetic. Let all these values be joined together into the value of character itself. Let there be convention. Let there also be originality and unique nobility. Let us have conservatism. Let us also have radicalism, and, above all, salvation. The forces of education and religion are both acquisitive as cause and result. They are also assimilative. They are both, furthermore, created, and are creative. Some principles and methods of religion seem to be antagonistic to each other. Some principles and methods of education, likewise, also seem, at times, to be antagonistic. Moreover, the principles and methods of both education and religion seem, at times and under certain conditions, to become even more antagonistic. But all and each are to be reconciled. Contradictions are to be abolished. They are to be united into the great categories. Life's dissonances are to be hushed, or heightened, indeed, into the noblest harmonies.

That rationalist moralist, or that moralist theologian, Professor C. C. Everett, has classified values as economic, bodily, values of recreation, values of association, character values, aesthetic values, intellectual values, and religious values. The classification is suggestive, the enumeration impressive. All of this quintette of values are to be united in the individual and in society.

Perhaps the most fitting illustration of this synthesis is to be found in the life and career of Pasteur,—Pasteur, a great scientist, a great philosopher, a great, the greatest, Frenchman, and a great humanist.

> Absolute faith in God and in Eternity, and a conviction that the power for good given to us in this world will be continued beyond it, were feelings which pervaded his whole life; the virtues of the Gospel had ever been present to him.[1]

[1] *The Life of Pasteur,* by René Vallery-Radot, translated from the French by Mrs. R. L. Devonshire, Vol. II, p. 312.

Of his last hours, it is said:

> How willingly they would have given a moment of their lives to prolong his, those thousands of human beings whose existence had been saved by his methods: sick children, women in lying-in hospitals, patients operated upon in surgical wards, victims of rabid dogs saved from hydrophobia, and so many others protected against the infinitesimally small! But, whilst visions of those living beings passed through the minds of his family, it seemed as if Pasteur already saw those dead ones who, like him, had preserved absolute faith in the Future Life.[2]

Into such a character, into such a service were joined together the greatest human and divine forces, in a fitting synthesis.

From such a completeness, there arises what might be called a sign of incompleteness, namely, a spirit of inquiry and of docility. Both education and religion are thus united. I recall that William Everett, son of Edward, once told me that, among his father's papers, he found a sheet on which the father had written words like these: "The Old Testament is the revelation of God, the Father; the New Testament, the revelation of God, the Son. Will there be a revelation of the Holy Ghost?" There may be no distinct third revelation. The present world is that revelation. The Holy Ghost is that revelation. But the spirit of inquiry is the prevailing spirit of both education and religion. I had a

[2] *Ibid.*, pp. 314-315.

classmate at Harvard, our first scholar, of whom another classmate said—himself an eminent physicist:

> The principle of his life may be stated in a remembered saying of his, to the effect that he would be happy to take ten degrees square of the heavens, make photographs of the stars therein and spend his lifetime in discussing it. Every problem that occurred to him seemed to him worth spending his lifetime over, and he was ready to do it, no matter what the drudgery connected with it. He never dropped it. He was never satisfied with what was already known about a subject. He wanted to know more about it. He was one of the few men who are born investigators. He was not one who wished to make a show in the world. He did not care whether the world ever knew what he was doing. With a broad, clear mind, capable of treating thoroughly any subject presented to it, he was willing for the truth's sake to sink himself in the one subject before him.[8]

This spirit of inquiry and of docility belongs to all great souls. I venture to quote here the record of such an experience of one of the greatest of American preachers. It is the experience of Horace Bushnell. If Brooks was the most representative, if Beecher was the most picturesque and poetical, Bushnell was the most philosophic, of the preachers of recent generations. I quote it because it is a wonderful example of style, and

[8] Harvard College—The Class of 1876, Tenth Report, p. 103.

because, also, it is a part of a sermon spoken to college men:

> Suppose that one of us, clear of all the vices, having a naturally active-minded, inquiring habit, occupied largely with thoughts of religion; never meaning to get away from the truth, but, as he thinks, to find it, only resolved to have a free mind, and not allow himself to be carried by force or fear, or anything but real conviction—suppose that such a one, going on thus, year by year, reading, questioning, hearing all the while the Gospel in which he has been educated, sometimes impressed by it, but relapsing shortly into greater doubt than before, finds his religious beliefs wearing out and vanishing, he knows not how, till, finally, he seems to really believe nothing. He has not meant to be an atheist; but he is astonished to find that he has nearly lost the conviction of God, and cannot, if he would, say with any emphasis of conviction that God exists. The world looks blank, and he feels that existence is getting blank also to itself. This heavy charge of his possibly immortal being oppresses him, and he asks again and again, "What shall I do with it?" His hunger is complete, and his soul turns every way for bread. His friends do not satisfy him. His walks drag heavily. His suns do not rise, but only climb. A kind of leaden aspect overhangs the world. Till, finally, pacing his chamber some day there comes up suddenly the question, "Is there, then, no truth that I do believe? Yes, there is this one, now that I think of it: there is a distinction of right and

wrong that I never doubted, and I see not how I can; I am even quite sure of it." Then forthwith starts up the question, "Have I, then, ever taken the principle of right for my law? I have done right things as men speak; have I ever thrown my life out on the principle to become all it requires of me? No, I have not, consciously I have not. Ah! then, here is something for me to do! No matter what becomes of my questions—nothing ought to become of them if I cannot take a first principle so inevitably true, and live in it." The very suggestion seems to be a kind of revelation; it is even a relief to feel the conviction it brings. "Here, then," he says, "will I begin. If there is a God, as I rather hope there is, and very dimly believe, he is a right God. If I have lost him in wrong, perhaps I shall find him in right. Will he not help me, or, perchance, even be discovered to me?" Now the decisive moment is come. He drops on his knees, and there he prays to the dim God, dimly felt, confessing the dimness for honesty's sake, and asking for help that he may begin a right life. He bows himself on it as he prays, choosing it to be henceforth his unalterable, eternal endeavor.

It is an awfully dark prayer, in the look of it; but the truest and best he can make, the better and the more true that he puts no orthodox colors on it; and the prayer and the vow are so profoundly meant that his soul is borne up into God's help, as it were, by some unseen chariot, and permitted to see the opening of heaven even sooner

> than he opens his eyes. He rises, and it is as if he had gotten wings. The whole sky is luminous about him. It is the morning, as it were, of a new eternity. After this all troublesome doubt of God's reality is gone, for he has found him! A being so profoundly felt must inevitably be.[4]

These words do well illustrate the spirit of inquiry and of docility which belong to the consummation of education and of religion.

Another of the fruits of education and religion relates to the evaluations of life. I now refer to a scheme or method for making this evaluation. At this writing, I am not so much concerned with what these values are, as I am with the way of getting at these values. For, what are the marks, or characteristics, of life's values? Would they not be somewhat as follows: universality, desirability, utility, lastingness? Assuming that this quartette of characteristics does represent a method of evaluation, let me ask whether education does not create and discipline the power of thinking which is universal, a power belonging to all space where mind may be, a power belonging to all time where any mind may exist. Does not education also give a power which all desire? Does not education give a power which is useful? Does not education create a treasure which "neither moth nor rust doth corrupt," which is more precious than gold, and more lasting than bronze? Furthermore, does not religion give a character which is

[4] *Life and Letters of Horace Bushnell,* pp. 58-59.

as broad as the limitless firmament, whose contents are cubical, a power which is much to be desired, which is the passport to kings' palaces and to the homes of the poor, and which is as lasting as the eternities? In his preface to *Mixed Essays,* Matthew Arnold says that the powers which contribute to building human civilization "are the power of conduct, the power of intellect and knowledge, the power of beauty, the power of social life and manners. Expansion, conduct, science, beauty, manners,—here are the conditions of civilisation, the claimants which man must satisfy before he can be humanised." [5] Apt and pertinent are these words, but they do not seem to take hold of the fundamentals, the foundations, the realities, deepest, broadest, lasting. Ruskin's *Seven Lamps of Architecture* give forth a purer and a more searching radiance, suggestive of nobler meanings and radiant with a guidance wiser and more compelling. These "lamps" belong to both education and religion. "The Lamp of Sacrifice" belongs to religion. The cross is its center. Sacrifice also belongs to education. It represents the lower giving way to the higher. "The Lamp of Truth" belongs to both education and religion. "I am the Way, the Truth, and the Life," declares Christ. *Veritas* and *Lux* are symbols of both forces. "The Lamp of Power" is the power of the Holy Spirit, the gift to the disciples, and the gift continued. Power is the purpose and the method of education. "The Lamp of Beauty" belongs to both. The beauty of holiness is the garment of the church. Beauty

[5] *Mixed Essays,* by Matthew Arnold, p. x.

is a supreme result of education. "The Lamp of Life" belongs to both education and religion. "I am come that you might have life and have it more abundantly." Education receives life, and receiving it, enriches it and gives it forth unto relations broader, deeper, higher, infinite. "The Lamp of Memory" belongs likewise to both. The continuity of character is the condition, the law, the force, the reward, of both religion and education. "The Lamp of Obedience" belongs likewise to the two. The commandments to be obeyed, the beatitudes to be heeded, the precepts to be followed, are the teaching of both Testaments. To make obedience to law the natural process of life is the principle of conduct, and is the aim and the method of education.

Another part of the fruitage I venture to describe as the personal contentments. In these contentments, I include three elements. The first is self-understanding. Such an appreciation, or depreciation, is the result of education. The great effect of knowledge is the assurance of one's ignorance. The effect of the coming of knowledge may be the advent, or the lingering, of wisdom, but certainly the effect represents, and is, the impression of one's own limitations. A second personal element is self-mastery. Religion thus disciplines its disciple. The will becomes fixed. Without stubbornness, it takes on firmness. The primary permanent choice, as the old phrase is, comes to its throne. Minor choices may contribute to the consummate result, but the major remains regnant. It embodies what the old theologians called "assurance." A third element of this personal contentment I shall call the belief that God has a good plan for His universe, and for every man in it. It is the belief found in the great phrase of the title of a sermon of Bushnell's, "Every Man's Life a Plan of God." It represents a confidence that, beyond all discordant and apparently contradictory phenomena, there is an intelligent and beneficent order. It is the faith found in the great lines of Lowell:

> Truth forever on the scaffold, wrong forever on the throne,
> Yet that scaffold sways the future, and, behind the dim unknown,
> Standeth God within the shadow, keeping watch above his own.

Further, in the consummation of the two great elements of our theme is found a deepening of the sense of mystery. As religion becomes more profound in its experience and broader in its content, as education becomes nobler in its scholarship and more human in its relations, so also the sense of the unknown becomes the more keen, the more present, the more intimate. Every transfer of the territory of the unknown to the territory of the known seems to enlarge the domain of the unknown. The more one knows, the more one wishes to know. As one goes upward toward the zenith of his knowledge, the wider becomes the horizon of mystery. The sense of mystery ever haunts, and haunts the reverent inquisitive soul in ever deepening measure. There are indeed five questions which seem especially to

[6] "The Present Crisis," Lowell's Poetical Works, Vol. I, p. 181.

surround and to penetrate our thinking. They are: (1) What is the essence of matter? (2) What is the extent of the physical universe? (3) What, or who, is God? (4) What, or who, is man? (5) What is man's existence after death? Of this quintette, the two first concern the outer world, and the remaining three concern man himself. Each of these problems changes its form from age to age. The provisional solutions given to each also change. For instance, a generation ago, the physicist and chemist said that the ultimate form of matter was the atom. To-day, both physicist and chemist declare that the ultimate form of matter is the electron, and that, within the electron, is found a universe—a universe of existence in which forces upon forces revolve in their ordained orbits, like the stars and planets of our firmament, "cycle and epicycle, orb in orb." In fact, a student in the Cavendish Laboratory, Cambridge, has just written me of a disc, the size of an American half-dollar, which contains a quarter of a million horsepower. Likewise, the extent of the physical universe is a problem long quickening man's mind. The astronomer's photographic lens brings to our vision points of light which the human eye has never seen, and perhaps never will see. But these points of light are apparently as real existences as are Jupiter and Sirius. Shall some other new and stronger lens still continue to bring to us the starlit banks of a universe apparently endless?

Such questions, quickening in themselves, are only exponents of questions deeper and more complex. Who and what is God? Who and what is man? Who and what is man after death? The problem of Job is still our problem, "Who by searching can find out God?" Who by thinking can find out what lies closest to man? Each represents the infinite mystery. Before that infinite mystery man bows in humility and reverence. He enters the temple of knowledge, but at its shrine stands the image of the Unknown. Do you remember Schiller's poem of the veiled image at Sais? Into the shrine in which stood the figure, veiled, the youth enters, eager, determined, passionate. He would approach the holy place. The guardian seeks to restrain him. In hot strength, he pushes on. He comes to the veiled figure. The veil he tears away. He looks, he sees—but, the poet declares, ever thereafter he was speechless. What did he see? one asks. God Himself? Destiny? One may draw a possible lesson that it is well for man to be the subject or even the victim of mystery. To know all might result in a kind of death.

But, from this consummation of mystery, there comes forth another completeness which is indeed not unknown, which is not veiled. It is the consummation of love. I refer to love as having two aspects, or relations, love as given and love as received. Both are bestowed and both are accepted. The word is also used in two great senses, love as a principle and love as an emotion, love as an act of the will and love as a mood of the heart. The New Testament makes a like discrimination, ἀγαπάω or φιλέω. Love as an act of the will stands for willing another's good. Love as a mood of the heart stands for an outgoing sentiment. The two may be united, and usually are. But also they may exist as separate conditions or forces. Together, they are the choicest fruitage of both education and religion. The teacher is to love the student in the sense of willing his good. Each love is of primary value. No teacher can prefer a student's ill; but it is possible for him to be indifferent to a student's good. If he be indifferent, his teaching is liable to be vain and useless. It is in his will for the student's good that he finds quickening of his zeal, strengthening of his patience, the upholding of his ideals, conditions which are essential for his work as a teacher. Likewise, the priest, in his service for his church, is inspired by his purpose of the well-being of its members, unto faithfulness "in season and out of season," in a Pauline mood and quest, which knows no ceasing. To be the object, too, of such a willing of love is hardly less glorious and satisfying than to be its active force. To be a member of a beloved class in school, or church, to know that the teacher and the priest are seeking for the best for all or for one, "this poor unworthy me!" is indeed a consummation which quickens gratitude, deepest and lasting. For the sentiment of love, given or received, one is indeed grateful. Let us rejoice in it. Let us pour it out toward other lives. Let it come into our own souls in floods of joy, and of deepest compensation and feeling. But, more formative, more constructive, of the best, more akin to the Infinite, dwelling with man, is the love which man gives to man, the love which man receives from God, the love which man gives to God, in a great *willing* of the best for all.

Such a love, be it said, in both senses, of the will and of the heart, belongs more and more to a college class, the longer the association of its members. Every college class, on its fiftieth anniversary, illustrates the truth. The members love each other as never before have they loved. The love is one of the happy consummations of their long career. The petty rivalries have ceased, the vain jealousies have ended. In the face of the death of most members, life takes on holier and more reverent meanings. In the stronger character of each survivor, each member looks his own destiny in the face. In mutual respect and admiration, each one finds that the members of the class have made a better contribution to life than seemed possible at the beginning of the half-century. Love blossoms forth for every fellow, in feeling and in choice. At a fiftieth anniversary, the beatitudes of education and of religion come to flower and to fruitage.

An impressive illustration of the value of love as a principle of action has recently been made public. An American asked the children of the schools of the world to name the twelve persons whom they regarded as heroes. In the definition of the hero were included the elements of nobility of character, fearless and self-sacrificing devotion to a great cause, and constructive work for humanity of a permanent character. As a result, these twelve men and women were named: Louis Pasteur, Abraham Lincoln, Christopher Columbus,

George Washington, Benjamin Franklin, Woodrow Wilson, Florence Nightingale, Joan of Arc, Socrates, John Gutenberg, David Livingstone, and George Stephenson. As one reads the list, and thinks about the names in it, does not one come to the conclusion that love as a principle of action, that love as devotion to a great cause, is the comprehensive keynote of the song of each man and woman? Love is the greatest thing in the world of man.

So far, in this chapter, I have spoken of the consummation of education and of religion as belonging primarily to the individual. It is, I hope, a not improper application. Yet, you and I know that it is an interpretation narrow. It should be made to have reference to the whole community and the whole commonwealth. Such an enlarged reference is natural and inevitable. The consummation of education and of religion, belonging to the individual, belongs also to the commonwealth. Syntheses, reconciliations, and harmonies are the gifts which the community receives in its devotion to religion and to education. The spirit of inquiry and the spirit of teachableness are the results which the commonwealth accepts from the lips of priest and of teacher. Just evaluations of life are made for the state by piety and by learning. The increased sense of mystery, brooding over all, is a beautiful lesson taught by the enlarging knowledge of the school, and by the holier creed of the church. The greatest thing in the world—of education and of religion—love, is the blessing and the fruitage of the divine religion and of the wisest education. Altruism is the whole atmosphere of each—to serve each and all is the common motive. Alike do the simple individual person and the whole commonwealth, the collection of individual persons, share in such consummations, richest, holiest, deepest, highest, universal, eternal:

> . . . The unknown good that rest
> In God's still memory folded deep:
> The bravely dumb that did their deed
> And scorned to blot it with a name;
> Men of the plain heroic breed
> Who love Heaven's silence more than Fame.

Like a piece of music, my theme turns back upon itself. I began in my first address with an allusion to the happiness of this historic spot as standing for the union of the forces of education and religion. I close with a still further assurance of a broader happiness. It is the happiness of a whole commonwealth in whose foundations these two forces were regnant and whose subsequent history is marked by their presence and their power. That happiness shall abide so long as these forces remain unimpaired and devoutly human; and these forces shall remain unimpaired and devoutly human so long as these hills greet the rising sun.

V

PARALLELS OF PROGRESS IN EDUCATION AND RELIGION [1]

THE first parallel in the progress of religion and education relates to the emancipation of each.

The nature of religion is determined by its doctrine of God. Changes in the nature of religion are measured, largely, by changes in its doctrine of God. The history of the emancipation of religion begins with the doctrine of a God feudal. It enters into and, so far as we are now concerned, ends with, the doctrine of a God democratic. The God monarchical is himself remote from man, but his activities do touch and influence man. He dwells in the infinities and immensities, but his scepter reaches out and touches the individual. The God feudal is partly remote and partly immediate. He is removed from those who are his foes, except as he comes forth to conquer them. Somewhat less remote is he from his friends, although with them his relation is not intimate. With special retainers, however, he may come into close fellowship. The God democratic is immanent. He dwells with those whom he rules.

With the God monarchical, religion spells obedience.

[1] Address delivered at the Oakland meeting of the Religious Education Association, 1915.

With the God feudal, religion spells service. With the God democratic, religion spells communion.

But religion has come to stand for a god whose name is not spelled with a capital. It has come to stand for a being impersonal, for a condition, for a state, for a general being. It has come to stand for the tendencies of things, for movements, for general constitutions, for a power, not ourselves, which makes for righteousness.

Religion, whether interpreted as standing for a personal God or for impersonal being, has thus passed forth into a certain degree of largeness, of indefiniteness, of vagueness even, which for better or for worse does represent emancipation.

The causes of this emancipation, which I thus briefly sketch, are somewhat as follows. The first lies in an increased respect for the reason of man. This respect begins with the founder of modern philosophy, Descartes. His *cogito ergo sum* indicates the fundamental value of human thinking. The emancipation is still further advanced, although on a different plane, by the critical philosophy of Kant and his followers, Fichte, Schelling, and Hegel. The scientific movement, too, of the last half-century, has still further deepened the appreciation of the human reason. As religion has become more rational, therefore, it has taken on the freedom of the free mind of the free man.

A second cause is found in pietism. Pietism, of course, represents the substitution of the emotions for the intellect, or for an adjustment of the relations of the two faculties, in which the feelings become superior and the intellect becomes subordinate. The freedom thus gained for religion is rather anarchistical, but it still deserves a great name.

The third cause lies in the growth of the natural and physical sciences, and especially in the science of biology and geology. In an apparent opposition of the conclusions of these sciences to the apparent teachings of the Bible, touching the creation and the development of man, and in the subsequent reconciliation of these teachings through a less superficial study, religion itself has been set free.

A fourth cause of emancipation lies in the general life of man himself. Man has become a practical optimist. Life's enrichments, life's enlargements, life's enjoyments, life's satisfactions and contentments have in the last two centuries become greater, deeper, broader, higher, finer. Such conditions could not but result in an increased sense of freedom of religion as standing for one of the fundamental elements of the life of him whose life has thus been made free.

A fifth cause lies in the increasing sense of the unity of the race and the races. This sense has also contributed to an increasing appreciation of the oneness of all religions. This oneness of all religions has come to rest upon a very broad basis, and this breadth of origin, of content, and of teaching results in a large sense of liberty.

Compared with the fact, and with the causes of the emancipation of religion, are to be placed immediately the fact and the causes of the fact of the emancipation of education.

The Roman idea of education is the training of the citizen; the Greek idea is the training of the artist; the Hebrew idea is the training of the religionist. The temple of education is founded upon a triangle which bears the three great adjectives, Hebrew, Greek, Roman. Of the forces which these nations have contributed, modern Western civilization is constituted. Out of these there came forth a further conception of education, which is to be named ecclesiastical. That conception stood for both the church and the priesthood. Its textbook was the prayerbook; its teacher's desk, the altar; its teacher, the priest. From such an early condition, education passed over into its feudal state. In its feudal state, education came to have close relationship to the family. From its ecclesiastical relations, and from domestic affiliations, education blossomed forth into the medieval university. That university was usually founded by a Papal bull, and its teachings were based upon, and its atmosphere permeated with, ecclesiastical dogma and influence. From this state education, with the rise of democracy, became itself democratic. Education found its place as a human force working, under human conditions, unto a human end. Nothing was foreign to it which belonged to man. It came to stand for complete individual and communal living. It represented the transmutation of knowledge into wisdom and of wisdom into character. It meant adjustment to environment. It came to mean the entrance of the individual into the traditions and experiences of the race. It came to stand for the cubical relations of character. It embodied the power to regulate the emotions, to guide the intellect, to quicken the conscience, to appreciate duty, to move the will. It came to stand for the apprehension and assimilation of all truth which belongs to humanity. It came to mean the knowing, the appreciating, the enjoying of the best.

The causes of emancipation of education are, be it said, not unlike those which were found working to effect the emancipation of religion.

The first cause lies in the enlargement of the field of life. All of life has become the province of the individual. Nothing human is remote from him. Education has become commensurate with life itself. Its terms are the terms of life. The freedom of life has therefore contributed to the emancipation of education.

A second cause lies in the enlargement of the field of natural science. The new fields of geology, of biology, of chemistry, of physics, are fields without boundaries. As they have been incorporated into the content of education their freedom has likewise been conserved to education itself.

A third cause lies in psychology. Man has become better understood, and the diversity of content and of force in his mind has also become better appreciated. Such variety, of course, spells emancipation. This psychological fact in the emancipation of education deserves to be compared with the worth of the critical philosophy of Kant and his successors in the emancipation of religion.

A second parallel in the progress of the two great forces of religion and education is found in the ultimate basis of authority belonging to each.

For twelve hundred years the basis of authority in religion was found in an organization, the church, the church Roman Catholic or Catholic. For no small part of Christendom that basis still obtains. But there came a time when, for the northern world at least, that basis was changed from an organization to a book. That book was the Bible. For many that basis still holds. Yet for some it was presently made evident that the Bible was like the "new presbyter," only the "old priest writ large." It also, beginning with liberty, ended in or approached unto intellectual enslavement, or at least restriction. From such a condition religion emerged to find its basis of authority in the reason of man. This reason is the arbiter, the standard, the judge—meaning for man what formerly the church or the Bible meant.

The reason of man as the basis of authority, broadly interpreted, takes on three forms. First, the feelings. The standard of the feelings was made the particular basis of authority. This standard had its special place in Schleiermacher, and especially in his doctrine of dependence on God. A second form of this authority was seen in the value placed upon the reason of man, and in a narrow interpretation of the reason. Perhaps no better exponent can be named than Ritschl. The third form is found in the current conception that the authority of religion is based on the personality of Jesus Christ, and especially on what he did. The model of this form is, "Do what Jesus did"; the battle cry is, "Do as Jesus would."

In education is likewise found a development of impressive similarity. The first authority in education, as in religion, is vested in dogma; the dogma which is to be accepted as true, and on the consequent duty of the dogma, on what is to be done. The standard of belief which is laid down for the conscience is conditioned by the truth to which the intellect gives assent. The authority of the church is repeated by the authority of the books. The *trivium* and the *quadrivium* of the medieval university are the standard to which all education is to conform. What was without the pale of the divine three or four was educational heresy. The authority of the book in education has largely been succeeded by the authority of man. This human authority has had, and still has, many elements and applications. It may, in general, be said that the progress of the different types of authority in both religion and education has been marked by the passing of mere information, by a lessening appreciation of knowledge, and by an increasing valuation of quickening or inspiring power, by a passing of the statical and the incoming of the dynamic.

In the development of these elements and applications are found still further parallels of the progress of religion and education. A third parallel, therefore, relates to the social emphasis. By the social emphasis in religion one means the conception that religion is to influence not only the individual but society. No single member of society is to be served or saved, but all members. Society is to be reconstructed and redeemed. No man liveth or dieth unto himself. His fellows are to be helped and blessed with himself. Society is not a mass of units unrelated, but an organism. The metaphor is not of physics, but of biology, of zoölogy. Relationships are vital.

A similar development occurs in education. It likewise has become social. The common school, the public school, are the proper adjectives. The state university is a phrase full of significance. The people have determined that education in higher as well as in lower relations shall not be committed to the chances of private initiative and of personal support. They have determined that, for the benefit of all society, every child shall be offered the highest and widest opportunities. They have recognized the truth of Washington's remark, made in his great farewell address, that in proportion as the institutions of Government are free it is important that the people be enlightened and educated. It is inferred that, as institutions have become extremely free, the people should be correspondingly enlightened and educated.

These two last-named parallels, the place of authority and the social emphasis, lead up to a fourth, the similarity in the progress of religion and education in their emphasis on the practical.

To all means and methods of the practical, religion through the church gives itself. Its social settlements, its guilds for teaching trades, its manifold associations, its clubs for lending money, for saving money, for sewing, these and all others represent the practical agencies of religion. The church has come to find its symbol more in the workroom than at the baptismal font or the sacramental altar.

Likewise in education the practical has become dominant. The grammar school represents vocational guidance; the high school becomes the technical, the technical the trade school, the academic college becomes the engineering department. Trade winds are the chief academic atmospheres. The purpose seems to be not to make scholars, but carpenters; not to make students, but journeymen. The aim of making a life has been supplanted by the aim of making a living.

To one further parallel I must refer: the similarity in the goal of religion and of education. Physicists write of the ultimate end toward which the universe is moving through unmeasured space in limitless time. Where that goal in the zones of space may be, or in what period in time's process that goal may be reached, they do not venture to prophesy; but that at some point in both space and time it shall be attained, they do recognize. Likewise religion and education have a goal. What is the goal of religion? May we not adopt the words of the prayer book, that it is a knowledge of God's truth in this world and in the world to come life everlasting? Or may we not more fittingly adopt the words of Christ and say that the goal is the purpose to have life and to have it more abundantly? Likewise, what is the goal of education? Is it not to know the truth, to know the highest truth, to know not in terms of intellect only, but in terms of heart and will and conscience, in terms of feeling, of experience, and of great choices? Is not the goal of education also life: life everlasting, life eternal, not simply in duration, but in the depths and heights and breadths of infinite being?

VI

WHAT CONSTITUTES A LIBERAL EDUCATION IN THE TWENTIETH CENTURY? [1]

THE question becomes one largely of definition. To help in the making of definition, I prefer to throw the question into a personal form. Who or what is the liberally educated man in this century? An education is liberal, because it makes a liberally educated man. If one know the result, one may easily trace out the cause. Yet, when one has transferred the problem to the human side, one soon and easily discovers that all difficulties are not elided. As Socrates said, when drinking the hemlock, "You may bury me if you can catch me." The trouble is to catch the man liberally educated and to hold him long enough to have a steady look at him.

The liberally educated man, we sometimes say, is the scholar. But each knows men who are scholars who do not embody an education of a liberal type. Knowledge, even knowledge broad, accurate, well ordered, does not always give a liberal education. I found one day in a noble laboratory of a famous university a woman who was breeding mice in order to

[1] An address given at the second mid-year meeting of the American Academy of Medicine, Chicago, March 25, 1909.

study certain inherited tendencies in coloring. I also met an eminent zoölogist in his laboratory on a morning who was intoxicating earthworms in order to study, under this excitement, certain activities of their nervous system. You know men who can discuss *Kai Gar* and the enclitic *De.* To neither the zoölogist nor the narrow Hellenist would one ascribe a liberal education. Is the grammarian an incarnation of the liberal type? You recall Browning's lines:

> Grant I have mastered learning's crabbed text,
> Still there's the comment.
> Let me know all! Prate not of most or least,
> Painful or easy!
> Even to the crumbs I'd fain eat up the feast,
> Ay, nor feel queasy. . . .
> So, with the throttling hands of death at strife,
> Ground he at grammar;
> Still, thro' the rattle, parts of speech were rife:
> While he could stammer
> He settled *Hoti's* business—let it be!—
> Properly based *Oun*—
> Gave us the doctrine of the enclitic *De.*[2]

I fear that the Grammarian was not a man of liberal education.

The liberally educated man, it is sometimes said, is the thinker; the man who can reason, judge, assess the truth at its proper value, relate truth to truth, infer a new truth, is the thinker. But there are men whose minds are as accurate in their movements as Babbage's calculating machine, who would never be judged guilty of having a liberal education. You know such men—

[2] Robert Browning, Vol. IV, pp. 250, 252. T. G. Crowell & Co.

orderly, precise, correct, their mental operations more regular than the movements of the heavenly bodies—but they are not liberally educated.

The man of a liberal education is a scholar, or at least is scholarly; he is a thinker, or at least is thoughtful, but he is also more than either the thinker or the scholar, in fact, more than both. This man liberally educated has entered the arcana of learning, yet he is not cumbered with or made heavy with the treasures which he bears forth. He is still intellectually alert. He has made himself a partner in humanity's life, but he has so shared that life as to create in himself a richer selfhood. He can judge truth and assess truth at a fair value. Every man, it is said, is either a Platonist or an Aristotelian. It may be truthfully said that the best man is both a Platonist and an Aristotelian. He is able to interpret like the one and to reason like the other. The man of liberal education has a mind deep in its fathomings without obscurity, high and noble without visionariness, broad without thinness. Its length and breadth and height are, like the City of God, equal. It is a mind, rich, yet not gorged, orderly without being merely an outline of thought, self-centered without arrogance, self-contained without assumption, strong without presumption, vigorous without coarseness.

United with this mind of the man of liberal education is a heart of sympathy. Sympathy liberalizes—sets free the mind and the man. He comes to have a fellow feeling with the universe; knowledge creates love. "I hate that man." "I thought you did not know him!" "I do not. If I knew him I should not hate him." As a fish has an instinct for water, the bird for air, so this man has instinct for man. "My brother" is his mood toward each. This man, if he be master of a single art or of a single science, ever has feeling with other masters in other arts and other sciences. He may be a physicist, but he knows the philosophy which underlies physics; he may be a philosopher, but he believes in the concrete. He is never vain; humility clothes him as a garment. He has powers of substitution, he is an altruist. He can see with others' eyes, feel with others' hearts.

This man is also a man of appreciation of the beautiful. The ministry of art is a very real ministry to him. Through it he finds a larger soul. In it he meets his maxima. A great poem lifts him, or great prose, like some passages in Newman or Burke. He feels, also, a great piece of music, or the dim spaces of cathedrals. This man has a mind to see and a heart to feel the grand, the beautiful, the sublime.

This liberally educated man is also a man righteous. He embodies the advice which Sir Walter gave to his son-in-law. Sir Walter, when dying, said: "Lockhart, be a good man!" He represents those qualities which Milton intimates: "Inflamed with the study of learning and the admiration of virtue; stirred up with high hopes of living to be brave men, and worthy patriots, dear to God, and famous to all ages." [3] They are

[3] *Tractate on Education.*

the qualities, too, which Wordsworth sings and embodies:

> So didst thou travel on life's common way,
> In cheerful godliness.[4]

Any lapse from moral goodness disintegrates not only the conscience, but the whole manhood. Man is one. He who breaks any law finds the stain and the sting touching every part of character. There is no ethical by-law. Each part is of a permanent constitution. Wrong produces self-consciousness in the wrongdoer, and in self-consciousness neither intellect nor heart is best or works best.

The man of liberal education lives, to use the phrase of Professor Palmer, in fullness of life. The phrase is the concrete expression for the remark of Christ: "I came that ye might have life and have it more abundantly." Every faculty acts, every function is complete. Reason *plus* sympathy *plus* appreciation *equal* fullness of life. Fullness of life equals the man himself of liberal education.

But now we approach the difficult part of the problem. The definition is easy to make. The conditions, forces, methods for securing this superb result—the man of liberal education—what are they? These conditions are more numerous, these forces more diverse, these methods more complex, than we have usually believed. We have been inclined to emphasize the content of the instruction contributing to the making of a liberal education. We have said that the classics, Latin and Greek

[4] *To National Independence and Liberty,* XIV. London, 1802.

especially, represent this content. Some have said that modern languages cannot give and others have said that modern languages can give, equally well, this precious product of a liberal education. Some have affirmed, comprehensively, that the linguistic content, not the scientific, of the curriculum promotes the great result. Others have affirmed that the scientific content is equally as efficient and enriching.

May we not say, in general, that each form of learning is good, and that each is useful? May we not say this without saying that each is equally good or equally useful? Is it not, in fact, unwise, as well as unpsychological, to say that this study or that is equally good or equally useful for all people? For, does not the value of the content of the study depend, in no small degree, upon the student, upon the intellectual nature of the man to whom this scientific or ancient classical or modern linguistic tuition is given? To one man may it not be true that Greek is the most potent force in securing a liberal education, and to another mathematics, and to a third chemistry? To some youths Greek may be a bar sinister, to others it may be the lifting of the gates of an earthly paradise. Content has value, but we have been inclined to overvalue its worth.

The method of instruction is also precious in the constitution of a liberal education. The method may be slovenly, careless, slow, wooden, stupid, stupefying. I have seen and heard teaching which deserved all these hard epithets. I presume that I have given in quite the same way such teaching. God forgive! I have also seen and heard and been the grateful object of teaching which was correct, comprehensive teaching, with a sense of relations, illuminated by illustrations, filled with a sense of movement, challenging to thinking. Such teaching, in any subject, is a most precious power in creating the liberally educated man.

The scientist may be inclined to depreciate Latin, but I know of the teaching of Latin which represents observation, accurate and prolonged, inference exact and necessary and as interesting as any experiment in any laboratory. I have heard the great Agassiz lecture. The world has, on the whole, discarded Agassiz's biological theories, but those who were his pupils believe in the methods of his teaching—vital, interesting, quickening, enlarging, creative. The method of instruction has value in constituting a liberal education.

Josiah Royce said recently, in an address given before the Committee of the American Association for the Advancement of Science:

> I insist then that one cannot in any general way distinguish between the educational offices of technical and professional studies on the one hand, and the studies productive of cultivation upon the other. I myself, for instance, ought to teach logic so as to make it professionally useful to future engineers and to future clergymen alike, and to any cultivated man as well, in case he can be induced to be for a while reflective. If I cannot do so, that is my defect as a teacher of logic. It is useless to condemn me to the vague task of

> simply so teaching logic as to exert a cultivating influence over people who have no trade and who have not yet chosen a profession. As a teacher of logic I ought to be required to appeal to anybody who chooses to try the value of my personal appeal to him, whether he is a professional student or a technician, a graduate or an undergraduate.[5]

A further contribution to a liberal education lies in what I may call atmospheres. An atmosphere is the spirit of a place. Atmospheres are the influences which come forth from very many sources to touch the life of the individual. The atmosphere of one home is of purity, gentleness, beauty, thoughtfulness, graciousness. Good taste, the conscience of the mind, prevails. The atmosphere of a neighboring home is not such. Contrast the atmosphere of Oxford with the atmosphere of some new college on new soil. Each has men of learning, each students of high purposes, and each a library. Each follows a scholastic régime and routine. What is the difference? One has an historic background and affiliations; one has noble architecture, is filled with traditions scholarly and personal, sympathetic with great movements, its annals replete with the names and exploits of great men. One embodies historic good taste and good tastes. Such conditions promise the great result of the liberally educated man.

I also want to be allowed to say that a force effective for a liberal education is religion. By religion I do

[5] "The American College and Life," *Science,* Vol. XXIX, March 12, 1909, p. 405.

not mean Christianity alone. I do mean, by religion, the relation which man holds to his God. That word he may spell with a small "g" or a large. The Being may be addressed as "who" or "what"; it may be a force which makes for righteousness, or it may be the unknown and the unknowable. But the infinite, the supreme, the Ultimate Being, the student seeks to bear a relation to, not of indifference, not of hardness of intellect or of heart, but of obedience, responsiveness, and coöperation. I have seen worshipers on the Ganges lift holy hands in prayer to the rising sun and bathe their faces in the golden light. I believe it was good for them thus to be and to do. The worship drew them out of themselves. It gave them affiliation with what they regarded as the divine. In a liberal education there must be this same element of the infinite. If an Italian painter three hundred years ago wished to paint an interior, he always left a door open or an outlook at some window. It saved the beholder from narrowness and closeness. A liberal education must open the mind to the supreme.

In any contribution to a liberal education in this century the point of view of the student occupies a significant place. Is the student a student? Has there not been a decline in the intellectual interests of college men? Has the decline in intellectual interests been as great or not as great as the increase in athletic sports? Are not an increasing number of men coming to college for what was formerly regarded as its by-products? Have we not changed the main purpose of the former time, the purpose of culture, of discipline, of efficiency for the by-products of that earlier time—fellowship and acquaintance? Have we not made the by-products of the earlier time take the place of the main result? Balzac once said: "Sometimes it seems to me that my brain is on fire. I shall die in the trenches of the intellect." How many men suffer such a conflagration or are in peril of such a death? In our interpretation of a liberal education we are discussing such questions as "Shall the teacher teach?" or "Should he lecture or should he hear recitations?" Such questions are important, but in the constitution of a liberal education, is it not equally important to include "Shall the student study?" Can there be any liberal education without the study of the student?

But as important as any one, and some would say as all, of these elements, is the teacher himself. Does not Goethe somewhere remark that one accomplishes most through personality? The force which creates a liberally educated man is a liberally educated man. Like makes like. Lincoln was educated by a few books and by life; Darwin by men and by himself. Pater says: "It is not so much what one thinks as the person who thinks that after all really tells." "Life therefore first," says John Addington Symonds. I have heard hundreds of graduates speak of their college course; most of them praise their teachers. But their teachers, and not the teaching in either content or method, is the special object of commendation. It is, therefore, the great personality, the teacher, great in learning and in thought, great in life, sympathy and appreciation, great in righteousness and goodness, great in relationship to the eternal, the supreme, the infinite, great in love, who helps to constitute a liberal education in this century.

Therefore, the content of learning, the method of instruction, the beauty and force of intellectual atmospheres, religion, the studying of the student, the personality of the teacher, all and each are the forces and conditions which help to make the liberally educated man, and therefore help to constitute a liberal education in the twentieth century.

VII

FORCES FOR THE WORLD'S RECONSTRUCTION [1]

TO-DAY is the result of yesterday. The past influences the present. Literature, art, law, philosophy, religion, history are among the noble avenues along which great forces move from the past to determine the present. And these avenues are open to the same forces in the present time, influencing the long future. Yet beneath, onflowing and ongoing, all these forces, mighty and constant as they are, seem to be but the expression of conditions more permanent and of forces possibly yet more fundamental. It is to some of these forces, as they themselves are to determine the future, I ask your thought.

I ask your thought in the largest relationship. For as I walked with the great Provost into this hall my thought was winged and went out to similar gatherings of this day, or like days, held over the world. For this day in the University of Pennsylvania is a day of the world, and for us the world problems are present, vital, even personal.

These forces, of which I am to speak, although briefly, are forces that, in my humble judgment, may

[1] Commencement Oration, University of Pennsylvania, June 20, 1917.

well be used in the construction or reconstruction of the world. One of these forces I shall call the Democracy of Human Nature. There is a civil democracy out of which and through which have come tremendous results for the happiness and the welfare of man. But there is a democracy, itself the parent of the civil type, still more significant and important. It is the democracy of human nature, the democracy of man himself.

You candidates for degrees know of the movement we call humanistic. It is the cause and the origin of great results in culture for man. You know and feel the movement we call humane, that blesses, ameliorates, and touches with balm the conditions of man. But broader, and more fundamental, and more lasting, is the movement that we call human: man himself, the ruler, the cause, the result of man.

The Greek gave us great results, and they were and are unique. The Roman gave us great results, and they were and are unique. The Hebrew gave us great results, and they were and are unique. And the Anglo-Saxon gave us the great cause and result of liberty, and it is unique.

But beneath, above, and around the results of the Greek, the Roman, the Hebrew, and the Anglo-Saxon is humanity itself. Above every race is man; above all nations is humanity.

"Why do you salute that man?" asked the attendant to the Pope of the Holy Father, in the streets of Rome hundreds of years ago; "he is a Jew." "But," replied the Holy Father, "he is a man." The democracy of man is a mighty force for us to use in the reconstruction of the damaged world.

With this also I join a similar force which I may call a Concert of Idealistic Souls—the union, the coworking of souls who are baptized in the waters of idealism. The soul! The technique, the technical, the efficient, the practical, have all their places. Let us confess, acknowledge, appreciate, and apply the truth of the remark.

In this time of happiness, in our full appreciation of such forces, let us realize the worth of the soul, of the intellect; yes, but not of the intellect simply; of the will, by all means, but not of the will alone; of the conscience, assuredly, but not of the conscience simply. Also, and possibly more than all, of the heart—of the heart that seems to be the expression of the soul, the heart that brings a lump into your throat when you see the flag, the heart that brings the tear into your eye when you hear certain songs, the heart that, as Pascal says, is deeper than the intellect.

Mr. Taft tells that one day when he was in the Philippines, lying upon his bed, sick in body, yet more sick at heart, there came to him over the plains and the mountains and under the seas a message from his classmates at Yale, gathered together on their twenty-fifth anniversary. There came to him this message, "Bill, we are with you." That is the concert of souls. That concert of souls comes to us quite as much as and possibly more as college people than to any part of humanity. It is the great freemasonry of hearts that represents that union, that coworking of great souls, mightier than nations or races, which is to help to repair this poor, wrecked old world of ours.

Let me also say, my friends, that the broader cause and helpfulness in this reconstruction lies in the domain that I shall call the imponderables, or the invisibles. We know what it is to weigh. We see the Fairbanks scales; we see yardsticks and meters. But the weights and the measures are not life's most important things; the things that cannot be weighed, that are impossible to measure, that no mortal eye can see, are life's most significant and lasting treasures.

Among them is the treasure and power of sacrifice. Sacrifice—sacrifice so beautiful, so holy, that it is no sacrifice at all. One could not do otherwise; the sacrifice that is life's whole and holy happiness.

A treasure, also, that cannot be weighed is the treasure of forgiveness. Oh, the nations are to have a chance of exercising forgiveness! I will not say forgetfulness; I do not say making the present like the past. I do say forgiveness—helping one who we believe has injured us into a better life.

You may have met Madame La Fontaine, of the family bearing this historic name. The other day, as she was speaking of her poor Belgian mother, unheard of for months, I said to her: "You must remember the words recorded in the Good Book, of Jesus Christ, the prayer, 'Father, forgive them, for they know not what they do.'" And quickly she turned upon me with a most proper reply: "Yes, but they know what they do."

Even if they do know what they do, we stricken ones must still be able to forgive.

With this quality there is to be joined something also which cannot be weighed, or measured, or counted, which we call honor. War is terrible. It may, at times, represent dishonor. But there is something more terrible than war. It is dishonor; it is contempt for truth; it is disloyalty to right; it is the degradation of the good. There is something mightier than material victories. It is honor and truth and right and duty. Those are the imponderables that are to weigh tremendously in the rebuilding of our world's future.

I also must speak of a force, and it is the last force of which I shall speak at this time, that shall help to remake our world. It is the force indicated in the great hymn we sang, and the force also intimated in the great verses we are still to sing. It is the belief in the Divine nature, the belief in God, the power of religion.

I am sure I speak to many who can join in the petitions of the Lord's Prayer that we have prayed together; I may speak to not a few who cannot join in a prayer to a personal God.

Whatever your religion in content or in form, yet religion may have the broadest content and the widest reference, going even beyond all realms of intellect. That power of a broad religion may and should influence the individual and help him to reconstruct in his day his world.

God, spelled with a capital or not; God, the universal in space, the eternal in time, present here as in the uttermost parts of the sea, to whom time is eternity and whose dwelling place is the light of the setting and the unsetting suns—that God, apprehended by your intellect, quickening your hearts, inspiring your consciences, moving your wills: that God is to be the greatest of all powers in the remaking of our world.

Therefore, I say to you candidates for degrees, to whom my simple thought is chiefly addressed—I say to you, use this quartette of forces as your contribution to the world for the next half-century in which your lives are to be passed: the Democracy of Human Nature, the Union and the Coworking of all Great Souls, the Weight of the Imponderables, and a Faith in God Himself. This quartette of forces you are to use. You are to use them in patience. It is a long road old humanity has yet to travel. You are to walk with willing, quiet feet along endless ways; and as you walk in patience you are to have visions.

This world of ours, it is said, is moving with unmeasured swiftness with other bodies through infinite space. You are to have a like thought of the swiftness of the ongoing of mankind. But also, and more, you are in this ongoing to think of the upgoing of man, the ascent of man from brute to man, from man to angel, from angel to archangel, up to the very foot of the throne of the eternal. You are to think and to sing that the world is rising, and that you are helping it to rise.

Therefore I feel like asking you candidates for degrees to take with me, so far as I have the right to ask you to take it, an oath not unlike the oath taken by the Athenian youth of the time of Pericles. That time was like the hour that this day witnesses in this house:

> I will never sully these sacred arms, nor will I forsake my comrades in the battle line of humanity. I will defend the world's shrines, although all other adventures fail; I will not leave the world less, but I will leave the world better and greater than I found her. I will obey my superiors and hearken to whatever laws the people have established, or hereafter shall establish. If any man aims to make void these laws or to disobey them, I will prevent him, and will defend these laws though I stand alone. I will honor the faith of my fathers. As witnesses hereto I call on the Gods.

May the oath of the Athenian youth of twenty-five hundred years ago be the oath of your soul on this day, in America, in the University of Pennsylvania.

VIII

IDEALS IN CITIZENSHIP [1]

MANY and diverse are the ways available for treating this, as every other, part of this rich program. After some deliberation I have decided that the least unworthy contribution to be made under this title would consist:

1. Of a statement of what the colleges have achieved in securing these ideals of citizenship.
2. Of what they may do under a complex social condition at the present time or in the immediate future.

In the Executive Department of the national government, of twenty-seven presidents, fifteen have been liberally educated. John Adams, John Quincy Adams, and Theodore Roosevelt received their education from Harvard; Jefferson and Tyler, from William and Mary; Madison, from Princeton; Polk, from the University of North Carolina; Pierce, from Bowdoin; Buchanan, from Dickinson; Hayes, from Kenyon; Garfield, from Williams; Arthur, from Union; Benjamin Harrison, from Miami; McKinley, from Allegheny (without graduating); and Taft, from Yale University. Monroe was a student in William and Mary, but left college to join

[1] Address at the 125th Anniversary of the University of Pittsburgh, February 27, 1912.

the Revolutionary army, and William H. Harrison was a member of Hampden-Sidney College in Virginia, but did not graduate. One-half of the vice-presidents have had a like advantage. Of our vice-presidents who have not served in the office of president, Burr and Dallas were graduates of Princeton; Hobart, of Rutgers; Gerry, of Harvard; Tompkins, of Columbia; Calhoun, of Yale; Richard M. Johnson, of Transylvania, in Kentucky; King, of the University of North Carolina; Stevenson, of Centre College, Kentucky; Fairbanks, of Ohio Wesleyan; and Sherman, of Hamilton College. Wheeler was for two years a student in the University of Vermont. The larger proportion of the members of the Cabinet have been liberally educated. Of the forty-one men who have filled the office of Secretary of State, twenty-seven have been graduated from colleges, and five others were in college for a longer or a shorter period. Jefferson and Randolph were graduated from William and Mary, and Monroe attended the same institution until the breaking out of the Revolutionary War, when he enlisted; Pickering, John Quincy Adams, Everett, and Bacon received degrees from Harvard; Madison, Smith, Livingston, Forsyth, and Upshur, from Princeton; Calhoun, Clayton, and Evarts, from Yale; Marcy, Olney, and Hay, from Brown; Webster, from Dartmouth; Legaré, from the College of South Carolina; Buchanan, from Dickinson; Fish, from Columbia; Blaine, from Washington (Pennsylvania); Frelinghuysen, from Rutgers; Foster, from the University of Indiana, where Gresham was a student one year;

Day, from Michigan; and Knox received a degree from Mount Union. McLane was a member of Newark College, Delaware, for three years; Seward was a graduate of Union after an interrupted course; and Sherman was in college two years. Also, it should not be forgotten, in the solution of the critical questions which Seward was obliged to make he especially relied on a president of Yale College, Theodore Dwight Woolsey; on Francis Wharton, a graduate of Yale in the class of 1839; and on William Beach Lawrence, a Columbia graduate of 1818. Of the Secretaries of the Treasury, Hamilton was a student in Columbia in 1774; Wolcott took his first degree at Yale, as did MacVeagh; Dexter, Richardson, and Fairchild, at Harvard; Gallatin, at Geneva, Switzerland; Campbell, Rush, and Bibb, at Princeton; Dallas, at Edinburgh; Taney and Thomas, at Dickinson; Woodbury and Chase, at Dartmouth; Ewing, at Ohio University; Spencer, at Union; Walker and Meredith, at the University of Pennsylvania; Cobb, at Franklin; Dix, at the University of Montreal; Fessenden, at Bowdoin, where also McCullough attended for two years; Bristow, at Jefferson; Folger, at Hobart; Shaw, at Cornell College, in Iowa; and McLane was for a time a student at Newark, Delaware, and Lot M. Morrill at Colby (Waterville) in Maine. One cannot forget, too, that in the office of the Secretaryship of the Treasury, it is the college graduate who has rendered the most conspicuous service. Robert Morris, who gave unique counsel in the management of the financial affairs of the country during the Revolution, declining the honor of becoming Secretary of the Treasury, pointed out Hamilton as the man best qualified to arrange the finances of the new nation. Hamilton was educated at Columbia. Chase, also called to the service of the nation in a crisis as great as that in which Hamilton served, was a graduate of Dartmouth in 1826; and Fessenden, Chase's successor, was a graduate of Bowdoin in the class of 1823. In this relation it is not unfitting to say that, in 1865, the man who was named chairman of a committee upon national taxation and revenues, and who did for the nation after our Civil War a service as important as Robert Morris rendered at the time of the War of the Revolution, was a graduate of Williams of the class of 1847—David A. Wells. Of those who have held other portfolios in the Cabinet somewhat more than one-half have received a liberal education.

The academic origin of the foreign representatives of our government is a history on the whole quite as honorable as the history of its legislative and executive functions. At the most important courts of the world we have been well served. To these courts, Harvard has contributed such men as the Adamses—father, son, and grandson—Elbridge Gerry, Rufus King, George Bancroft, Caleb Cushing, Motley, James Russell Lowell, Bancroft Davis, Robert Todd Lincoln, Charlemagne Tower, and Joseph H. Choate. It may be said too, in passing, that George Downing, a graduate of Harvard in the class of 1642, went to England and became, besides filling other important posts, a minister to Holland under Cromwell and Charles II. His name is perpetuated in Downing Street and Downing College. Yale also has given to our diplomatic service such men as Edwards Pierrepont, Joel Barlow, Cassius M. Clay, Peter Parker, William Walter Phelps, Andrew D. White, Eugene Schuyler, Wayne MacVeagh, and Stanford Newel; Columbia, such citizens as John Jay, Hamilton Fish, Stewart L. Woodford, and Oscar S. Straus; William and Mary, such statesmen as Jefferson, Monroe, and William C. Rives; Princeton, such sons as George M. Dallas, William L. Dayton, and George H. Boker; Dartmouth, such a scholar as George P. Marsh; and Brown, Ambassadors like President Angell and John Hay.

Such is the record—a record enlightening to the mind, moving to the patriotic conscience, and quickening to all collegiate endeavor.

But what of the present and of the future? For the Victorian age has, like a late-staying guest, finally passed out. The era of good feeling has vanished. The social quietness, the mediocre respectability, the timid decorousness, the life which was comparative because it was not superlative, the era of ideals, but of ideals so low that they did not create despair in trying to attain unto them, nor so high that they quickened great enthusiasm in the probability of reaching them, have all gone, both in England and America. We have passed from the age of statics into the age of dynamics. We have come into the age of force, forces, and of forcefulness. We have entered from conditions into movements. The age of individualism becoming aggressiveness; of aggressiveness becoming unrest; of unrest becoming social and industrial reformation, of reformation becoming social and industrial revolution; of revolution tending toward anarchy, seems at last to have come upon us.

Now, in this condition, sketched so imperfectly in broad lines, *What can the colleges and the universities do to make things better?* The question is significant. For the higher education does not desire to nurse a fugitive and cloistered virtue. It desires to serve—as it ought to serve—the highest, broadest, deepest, and most enduring interests of man.

The higher education can help men, its students, to look at facts as they are, and to weigh the evidence which these facts present. Of course, the colleges have always been seeking to achieve this result. The colleges have always been trying to teach this significant fact that 2 and 2 make 4. A significant fact, indeed, for always there are some in the community who are trying to squeeze 2 and 2 into 3, and an equal number who are trying to enlarge them into 5. In the training of this power of looking at facts as they are, and in weighing evidence, lies the worth of education. But the college has a special duty laid upon itself to transmute this general obligation into a duty specific and particular. For to the great social and industrial facts one is specially liable to be blind. The facts are not like the reforms of the Gracchi—remote. They are immediate. So close are they that it is difficult to see them as they are; to interpret their relations; to point out their significance; or to lay down a course of conduct based upon their meanings. But they are pregnant with new births for men. Their nearness generates passion. Truth's white light has a small chance for shining. For better or for worse, for destruction or for construction in this difficult environment, they must be interpreted. Such interpretation the college can inspire its men to seek to make. It should help men to see these phenomena sanely, and to see them whole.

The college, further, may give greater place to what I call the human sciences. These sciences include history, economics, government, and sociology. The increase in the emphasis laid on these subjects has, in a score of years, been vast. It is hardly possible to exaggerate the increase. It is not for me to depreciate the worth of the natural sciences, either as intellectual disciplines or as revelations of the wonders of the creative process. Let the natural sciences have their full and adequate place. But I do believe that the social and industrial conditions demand that college men shall go forth with some understanding of the complexity and seriousness of these conditions. For the complexity and seriousness of these phenomena are giving rise to social and industrial quackery. Who is the quack? He is the man who has a ready-made diagnosis of disease and a remedy no less ready-made for its cure. The social quack abounds. The quack of the Single Tax, the semi-quack of municipal ownership, are plentiful. "Go to, now! *This* is the cause of all your ills. And *this*, without fail, will save you." As if any patent medicine could save. The people are misled. Harm results. The disease spreads. The patient grows worse. Where can help be found? I know too well the imperfections and weaknesses of the colleges. But if help is coming, it must come in accordance with the great human laws which are as real as, though harder to understand than, the great laws of nature. These laws, these principles, of social, political, civil, and industrial well-being are studied, considered, related to each other in the colleges and universities. The men who have been students of these laws and principles are above all others best qualified to apply these laws to the body politic and social. Humanity goes on repeating its experiments which have failed. Its memory is short. The colleges stand for accumulated thought. They represent and present the history of human experimentation. The colleges should save men, at least somewhat, from repeating their great social errors and mistakes. The result of all the help the colleges can give will indeed be poor enough, but these results are the most precious and effective which humanity in its present stage of cultivation can attain unto.

It is a happy augury that no subjects are so popular in the American colleges as these "Human Sciences." Students appreciate their importance and are touched by the appeal which they make to present-day life. Though lacking the disciplinary value of the exact sciences and mathematics, though lacking, also, certain interpretative values of the classical languages, they do give, if taken up subsequent to a proper study of the exact sciences, an enlargement and enrichment of the mind of the student and a peculiar inspiration to become a worker in a world of work.

But there is a further method which the colleges may use in overcoming the anarchistic tendencies of the social and industrial movement. This method consists in the establishment of departments of the Human Sciences, for the special advantages of men of mature years who are especially interested in these subjects and who have not been able, by reason of their domestic and other limitations, to give themselves a proper education. This suggestion is by no means new. It bears memories of movements which have a somewhat prolonged history. The workingmen's colleges of fifty years ago, of which the great Maurice and the versatile Kingsley were founders and sponsors and supporters, embody the same noble idea. To-day no better exponent of the movement is found than is incarnated in Ruskin College at Oxford. The difficulties in laying such a foundation are neither few in number nor slight. The ordinary members of a college faculty are seldom able to undertake such a task. Their duties are altogether too heavy for any such permanent additional service. For a brief time they may take such work upon themselves, but not as a lasting service. A special staff, therefore, is to be organized; and such a staff, competent in mind and conscience, is hard to secure. Furthermore, many men desiring to become students are found to lack a proper general education. They have not the intellectual qualifications to take up special social studies, than which no subjects are more complex. Their eagerness and enthusiasm go a certain way—with some men, a long way—in overcoming the lack of disciplined mental power; but enthusiasm cannot be accepted as a substitute for a trained intellect. Though, therefore, every college may well consider the question of offering such courses, especially if placed in the midst of an urban community, yet the outlook is not bright for results either comprehensive or lasting.

I am also inclined to believe that the regular college officers may make a most effective use of their own wisdom and counsels in securing the great end of social and industrial peace. It is a perilous thing for a professor or president to give specific advice to a new student regarding the choice of a calling. Principles he may lay down. Their application should be committed to the man who must bear the responsibilities of the choice. But officers should feel free to point out, and perhaps should do more than to point out, the opportunities open in social service as a vocation, or open even as an avocation. I have known the head of an institution of five hundred students to make plain suggestions to hundreds in respect to a life's calling. Jowett, of Balliol, was supreme master in such guidance. It is at this point that the college may render especially effective service. I have referred to the lack of wise leadership in the great social movements. Cannot the colleges do more in securing such leadership? Cannot the college train men into such intellectual power and with such human sympathies that its graduates shall feel the impulse to enter into such movements and be able to give wise leadership? Many men in college are, as I have said, more or less socialistic. If they, entering life and taking part either formally or informally in these tremendous affairs, can keep their judgment large and clear, they should in time be able to give great help in offering right direction to these movements unto the happiest results.

IX

WHAT STUDIES MAKE MIND? [1]

An Answer Made through the Harvard Law School and Many Colleges

THE studies that make mind and the worth of the tests which are applied to the mind, made or making, form two of the most serious and complex questions of the higher education. An answer, at least of some worth, to the two questions may be found in the colleges and in a typical professional school.

The method of investigation for making answer in this instance was simple. The Secretary of the Harvard Law School compiled for me a list of the graduates of that School who, for forty-two years, from 1880 (the year of their establishment) to 1921, had received final scholarship honors. The list numbers seven hundred and nine names. The names found in the annual record go from four, as in 1917, to thirty-four, as in 1902. These men are graduates of no less than one hundred and four colleges. In turn, the officers of these colleges furnished at my request a full and detailed statement of the studies and the honors of their graduates who subsequently took honors at the Harvard Law

[1] Published in the *Harvard Graduates' Magazine,* and used at Phi Beta Kappa and other academic meetings.

School. This Law School was selected for comparison for several reasons, one being that it has the longest record of honor men of any American professional school.

To the primary questions of the nature of the forces for the making and testing of mind, the facts thus presented do not allow the giving of an absolutely conclusive answer. Perhaps no conclusive answer is possible. But I do hope that the following pages, interpreting the material thus offered, will give some light for the making of a proper answer. Certainly the material thus offered is at least unique, whatever may be the worth or worthlessness of the interpretation of it.

The two score and two years covered represent a pregnant period in American and world education. It is a period marked by the transfer of education from a pretty fixed and narrow content to a curriculum distinguished by the introduction of the new studies of the natural and physical sciences and of the newer humanities. The seven years, too, which each individual member of the group had spent in his liberal and professional education represent the most intellectually formative period of his whole life. The resulting condition is, therefore, of significant interest to those seeking to discover what are the forces best fitted to give an education and training which most adequately prepare for the study and for the practice of a great profession. Through a proper inference, moreover, intimations are offered concerning the character of the educational forces fitted to discipline the mind of man for securing high general purposes as well as for achieving aims strictly professional.

Before entering into the formal and detailed statement of these facts or into an interpretation of them, it is proper to ask whether honors conferred by the Law School of Harvard University upon its graduates are a fair and just test of intellectual power and progress? These honors are assigned as a result of examinations held upon the studies pursued in the School and passed with "distinguished excellence." These studies comprise technical subjects usually taught in a law school, and also subjects having general relationships.

In the three years of his studentship at law, each man takes examinations in no less than seventeen subjects, and the actual period of examination covers a total number of no less than seventy hours. The directions or suggestions given to the student printed at the head of each set of questions represent rather impressive elements and qualities of the whole examination process. I quote from the papers set for June, 1922:

> Give reasons in all cases. Do not be diffuse, nor too brief. One or two pages will usually be sufficient for a good answer.
>
> Give (a) your conclusion; (b) your reasons. . . . Credit will be given for concise and accurate English; no credit will be given for any answer more than two pages in length.
>
> Four hours. Give reasons for each conclusion.

> The whole chain of reasoning should be stated, including every proposition of law and the justification for it and the method of applying it to every case; but the limit for each answer is three pages.
>
> Reasons must be given in all cases, but terseness in presentation is a merit. . . . Assume that objects and exceptions are properly taken.
>
> State your conclusions first, then your reasons.
>
> Read the whole paper before answering any question. Credit will be given for concise and accurate English; do not write more than thirty pages in all.
>
> Twenty-five pages is a suitable maximum.[2]

The questions themselves form a series of problems. They are such problems as a lawyer meets in his practice. They represent, in fact, the "case system" raised to its highest power.

These intimations indicate clearly and strongly the severity of the logical reasoning required in answering the questions proposed. To pass such examinations upon these subjects, set at the close of each year, demands a speedy and prompt command of one's intellectual forces. It exacts accuracy of discrimination in the separation of the essential from the incidental, of the fundamental from the derived, of the necessary from the accidental. It commands power of general reasoning. It demands a mastery of logical method and a sense of proportion of intellectual values. It requires an intellectual force, vigorous, trained for immediate

[2] Papers used at the Annual Examinations in Law, held at Harvard University, June, 1922, pp. 8-48.

use. It also presupposes soundness of nerves and of general health, as well as fullness of knowledge. The examinations stand, in fact, for the most effective use of the full intellectual power of the better graduates of the better colleges. It is through such forces and conditions that honors are won. What may be called the "oratorical mind" has no place. The inference is inevitable that the honor men of the Law School of Harvard University, of each year, are men of the best education. They do possess the qualities which the college of liberal learning seeks to create and to nourish in its graduates.

In passing, it may be added that each professor in the Law School reads, each year, from twelve thousand to twenty thousand pages of manuscripts. These manuscripts cover examinations held at the close of each academic year. These pages represent from five hundred to six hundred "blue-books." One professor tells me he can read on the average three books an hour. It requires no long process in mathematics to prove that such reading and assessment occupy practically a month of the working time of each year. This work, be it said, is not delegated to subordinates.

All students entering the School are graduates of colleges. Many of these colleges, not all, are of historic foundation, the more amply endowed and equipped. The graduates therefore have pursued studies of a comprehensiveness, worth, and variety which belong to the more enriching curriculum. It is, however, only with the courses of study which the honor men themselves have pursued in their undergraduate career that I am now specially concerned. Of the one hundred and four colleges considered, I am, of course, obliged to make a selection. I select six which are perhaps as representative of the diverse conditions of geographical and scholastic worth as could be made. The six are Yale, Princeton, Dartmouth, Knox, Leland Stanford, and Harvard. Other colleges may be equally representative, but none more.

Of these colleges I am unable, of course, to give full statements regarding the undergraduate studies of each man. At this point, too, selection must be made.

Out of the fifty-five honor men who entered the Harvard Law School from Yale in the forty-two years, I select three, a member of the Class of 1902, a member of the Class of 1911, and a member of the Class of 1915. The member of the Class of 1902 took, in his Freshman year, these five studies: Greek, Latin, Mathematics, French, English. In the Sophomore year, he also took Greek, Latin, and French; Physics was substituted for Mathematics; and, in addition to English, what is called Rhetoric was taken. In his Junior and Senior years he took Philosophy, Economics, History, German, and Spanish, and, in addition, in the Senior year, French, returning to the study which he pursued in the first two years. The member of the Class of 1911, in his Freshman year, took Greek, Latin, History, English, and Chemistry. In his Sophomore year, Greek, English, and History were repeated, and German and

Philosophy and Rhetoric added. In his Junior year, his studies were Economics, English, Geology, History, and Philosophy. In the Senior year all these studies were repeated, and an addition made of Physics. The member of the Class of 1915, in his Freshman year, took Latin, German, English, Chemistry, and History. In his Sophomore year, the studies were identical, excepting that Greek took the place of German, and Biology the place of Chemistry. In his Junior year, his studies were Greek, English, History, Philosophy, and Anthropology. In his Senior year, English, History, and Philosophy were continued, Latin was substituted for Greek, and Music for Anthropology.

Princeton sent to the School, in this period, twenty-seven graduates who became honor men. The undergraduate record of five representatives of this number is as follows. In point of time, the first honor man was a member of the Princeton Class of 1883. His subjects, for the long-ago period, were Greek, Latin, English, Mathematics, Philosophy, the Science of Religion, Chemistry, Astronomy, Politics, and Economics. The second honor man, coming seven years later, of the Class of 1890, was graduated having Latin, Greek, French, Mathematics, Physics, Politics, Philosophy, English, Ethics, Astronomy. The member of the Class of 1902 took Latin, Greek, Italian, Metaphysics, History, Mathematics, Psychology, Ethics, Economics, and Philosophy. The member of the Class of 1909 took Latin, Greek, Mathematics, Philosophy, English, History, Politics, Economics, and German. The member of the Class of 1916 took Latin, Greek, Mathematics, English, German, Philosophy, Physics, Astronomy, and Politics.

For fifteen years of the period, Dartmouth College gave to its men more largely of the Ancient Languages and Mathematics than many colleges. Of the seven honor men at the School, graduates of the classes between 1879 and 1894, the typical college record is a classical course having its basis in Latin, Greek, and Mathematics. The Dean of the Faculty writes me that, up to the year 1894, it was necessary for a man to put his principal work in the Ancient Languages and Mathematics, but that, after this date, they were able more or less to make selection, and "B. S. candidates" with the basis of Ancient Languages began to prepare for the Law School. Under this new régime, the record of three men is representative. Of a member of the Class of 1900, it is said: "Very high graduate student: Phi Beta Kappa; Ancient and Modern Languages, History, Political Science, and Economics." Of a member of the Class of 1906, it is said that he had Latin, French, German, Mathematics, Economics, Political Science; and of a member of the Class of 1912, it is found that he returned to the earlier form of Greek and Latin, adding French, Economics, and Political Science.

The fourth college of the representative list is Knox, a New England college planted on the rich Illinois prairie. In this period, Knox sent five men who took honors in the Harvard School. Four of the earlier graduates emphasized Latin, Greek, and English. English, in fact, was taken throughout the whole course. Briefer studies are found in the sciences, both natural and human. History, Philosophy, and Economics are also included. The last graduate, however, took no classics, but did take French and German, with the usual studies in Mathematics and English. In fact, his course belongs to the order of Bachelor of Science rather than to that of the Bachelor of Arts. It is noted that each of the five men excelled in debate and in English. For the Dean writes that "Knox has always given considerable attention to public speaking and debate."

Of the six men sent by Stanford, I give the record of two, each record including Latin, Greek, French, English, and History. Among the other studies are Philosophy, Economics, German, Zoölogy, and Botany. A major subject taken by the two men was Latin, and also History taken by one.

Of the three hundred and forty-one honor men who received their first degree from Harvard College, I choose seven. Each of these seven "majored" in Languages. History, too, was taken by each of the seven. Five took Mathematics and Science, six Economics and Mathematics, four Government, and three Fine Arts. A study of all the Harvard records available shows that, during the forty-two years, 2248 courses in Modern Languages were taken. History follows with 1177 courses, Ancient Languages with 904, Economics with 829, Science with 805, Philosophy with 603,

Mathematics with 438, Government with 398, and Fine Arts with 208.[8]

I wish it were possible to give a statement of the studies taken in the one hundred and more colleges by each of the seven hundred and more men. But I do venture to say that the few whom I have selected are representative. The general qualities and fundamental elements belonging to the men chosen from the six colleges, Yale, Princeton, Dartmouth, Knox, Leland Stanford, and Harvard, characterize the entire number.

Of course, in making any evaluation of these or of other studies, as forces of intellectual discipline, it is clear that many questions, professional and elementary, spring to the mind.

One question, both fundamental and superficial, is this: whether the men who normally take Latin

[8] The whole statement, even in tabular form, is impressive:

Years	*Anc. Lang.*	*Mod. Lang.*	*Fine Arts*	*Sci.*	*Hist.*	*Govt.*	*Econ.*	*Math.*	*Phil.*
1880-1890 (72 men)	361	304	42	216	243	19	117	195	177
1891-1897 (72 men)	213	529	44	207	251	27	169	89	102
1897-1903 (72 men)	131	604	67	143	259	123	173	85	117
1903-1910 (72 men)	111	469	36	145	253	128	225	35	95
1910-1921 (53 men)	88	342	19	91	171	101	145	34	112
Totals	904	2,248	208	805	1,177	398	829	438	603

The records of ten men are lacking, one man's name is lacking in 1881, and eighty of the men did not take full courses in Harvard College.

The above estimate is based on seventy-two men in each of the earlier periods, the number of men included in the first decade.

and Greek, as do most of these men, as undergraduate studies, are men of the type who also normally select the law as a profession. Does the discipline of the Ancient Languages naturally incline such students to the study and the practice of the law? Or, more definitely, does the pursuit of the Ancient Languages give a definite and distinct education for winning honors in the Law School?

It is clear, in my judgment, that the men who pursue the Ancient Languages as their principal undergraduate studies are naturally and normally the men who adopt the law as a profession. For these studies, like the profession itself, represent subjects solid in content, demanding patience in their pursuit, disciplining intellectual accuracy, devoid of immediate and striking effects, free from picturesqueness, representing a large sense of relationship, and fraught with problems diverse and significant. If students of a philosophical type normally enter the ministry, if men of a psychological and scientific type normally enter medicine, and if men of an executive and mathematical type normally enter business or the profession of engineering, men of the more solid and diverse intellectual type enter the law. The drift is plain. The discipline of the studies, moreover, emphasizes the natural movement. Latin and Greek, and all linguistic studies, train the solid parts of character, tend to give soberness (and some would say grayness) to intellectual atmosphere and movement. It is also evident that the pursuit of such studies in the undergraduate years cannot fail to train students to win honors in the graduate school of law. For as Professor Wambaugh of the Law School says:

> The lawyer's needs with reference to language are two: first, he needs an accurate taste for differences in shades of meaning, in order that he may frame formal documents properly and may construe with a critic's skill constitutions, statutes, wills, and contracts; and, secondly, he needs a rapid use of a large vocabulary, in order that he may acquit himself creditably before judge and jury. Such taste and such command of language can best be attained at present by the study of languages other than English. As the Greeks gained a mastery of their own language without learning any other, it seems clear that a thorough mastery of English can be gained without studying ancient or foreign languages; but the fact remains that at present it is through the study of other languages that the best command of English is obtained. Only in studying other languages do we have patience to master details of grammar, the history of words, shades of meaning. That is to say, only in mastering another language are we willing to study words with a microscope. From the study of other languages, then, comes the ability and the tendency to be accurate. Further, the translating of other languages into English, especially when the translating proceeds rapidly at sight, as in the modern methods of

instruction, is the best possible means of obtaining a ready and graceful vocabulary.[4]

The testimony of Professor Wambaugh is reënforced by the interpretation given by the present Dean of the School, Professor Pound:

> There is no better way for the student to train himself in the choice of the very word that will fit his thought than by translation from Latin and Greek. Such habits are worth more to the lawyer than all the training which a modern school may hope to impart.[5]

The testimony, therefore, based on the experience of students who have followed the fundamental curricula, as giving the best preparation for the successful study of the law, is clear. This testimony is that the course having as its chief elements the Ancient Languages and Mathematics as the principal parts, with Modern Languages, the Sciences, History, Economics, as subsidiary studies, form the best preparation.

This conclusion is the very conclusion which John Stuart Mill declared in his enduring Rectorial address, given at St. Andrews in 1867. One need not go as far as Mill goes, yet one can go a certain distance. Mill says:

> The only Languages, then, and the only Literatures, to which I would allow a place in the ordinary curriculum, are those of the Greeks and Romans;

[4] *The Best Education for a Lawyer,* an address by Eugene Wambaugh, LL.D., Professor of Law, Harvard, p. 5 of printed pamphlet.
[5] *Pamphlet of the American Classical League,* July 3, 1922.

> and to these I would preserve the position in it which they at present occupy. That position is justified, by the great value, in education, of knowing well some other cultivated language and literature than one's own, and by the peculiar value of those particular languages and literatures.[6]

Mill also says:

> No modern writings come near to these, in teaching, both by precept and example, the way to investigate truth, on those subjects, so vastly important to us, which remain matters of controversy, from the difficulty or impossibility of bringing them to a directly experimental test. To question all things; never to turn away from any difficulty; to accept no doctrine either from ourselves or from other people without a rigid scrutiny by negative criticism, letting no fallacy, or incoherence, or confusion of thought, slip by unperceived; above all, to insist upon having the meaning of a word clearly understood before using it, and the meaning of a proposition before assenting to it;—these are the lessons we learn from the ancient dialecticians. With all this vigorous management of the negative element, they inspire no skepticism about the reality of truth, or indifference to its pursuit.[7]

The testimony thus given is not new. The evidence which I offer is simply a confirmation of what soberminded educators have long believed and impressively

[6] "Rectorial Addresses," University of St. Andrews, pp. 30-31.
[7] *Ibid.,* p. 37.

affirmed. The ground which Mill takes in his great address is one which he also affirms in his no less great and earlier essay on "Liberty."

Going along with this general induction are several inferences both positive and negative, quite as pregnant in significance and impressive in interest. A most important inference relates rather to the condition or result, than to the content, of study. This inference is that the chief worth of the college in preparing candidates for high success in the study of the law lies in giving a thorough intellectual discipline. It lies in the power of thinking. As Professor Wambaugh has also said:

> In the fitting school and the college, the general purpose of study, unlike the general purpose of study in childhood, is to give to the mind strength, alertness, refinement, and, in short, culture.[8]

It lies, in fact, not in information, not in the merely knowing of a subject, but in the method of study. The value is found, as a Professor of Law in the University of North Dakota has said:

> Training, not information, should be the primary end sought in collegiate preparation for the study of law. The items of information that are acquired in college will, in the course of time, be largely forgotten, and even though they should not be forgotten they will often become out of

[8] *The Best Education for a Lawyer,* an address by Eugene Wambaugh, LL.D., Professor of Law, Harvard, delivered June 15, 1892.

date. The training of the mind in the process of education, however, develops mental habits which for good or for evil affect the individual's work through his entire life. The mental habits of alertness, accuracy, thoroughness, and persistence are far more useful than the items of information dealt with in the pre-legal work. If acquired in the pre-legal work, these habits not only enable their fortunate possessor to do his law-school work well, but also, through the habit of effective application to whatever he undertakes, bring him success through his entire career.[9]

The chief worth of the college course lies in teaching the student the use of his tools. These tools are his human equipment. The great value consists in giving to himself the power to think, to think broadly without shallowness, to think deeply without narrowness, to think highly without visionariness. Students of Dean Ames recall the constant emphasis he placed on the value of thinking. Students, to-day, are more inclined to undertake executive work than to meditate. It is meditation which prepares one to pursue a professional course, be it theological, or medical, or legal, with satisfaction and hopefulness. Some students are more inclined to elect "activities" than activity. The "activities" are more desirable than was the loafing life of half a century ago. For loafing was the chief

9 "The Best Pre-Legal Studies," by Lauriz Vold, Assistant Professor of Law, University of North Dakota, published in the *Quarterly Review of the University of North Dakota,* Vol. VIII, No. 1, July, 1918, p. 388.

resource of men who did not care to study. But, at present, "activities" which are indeed a good discipline for the executive and administrative powers of the student, are not a good discipline for the intellectual. The student finds the richest result coming from hard intellectual work, covering long periods of time, concentrated upon a few subjects pursued with unrelenting constancy and vigilance, and with all possible enthusiasm—work calling out, and therefore creating, intellectual forces; work demanding resource, discrimination, and ever done with thoroughness. The testimony of the records of the seven hundred graduates is that the "activities" of the college, even if numerous and stalwart, and closely woven together, do not make up into the best scholastic gown, a gown for long and constant wearing. The testimony is that the soft courses do not give that hard-headedness which experience finds belongs to all greatly successful men. The testimony is that the snap courses do not nourish prolonged and constant and concentrated power of thinking, thinking which characterizes the ablest members of every profession. The evidence, based upon the study of the careers of these seven hundred men, is that the studies, begun in their freshman year, were usually pursued in the sophomore, that the studies begun in the junior year were also followed in the senior. Mrs. Humphry Ward, writing of her early life, says that her study of the origins of early Spain lasted about two years, years of insistent, arduous work, and that it was the only thorough discipline she ever had. It is such discipline, the result of insistent, arduous work, that best fits the college student to do similar work in the law school and to crown his work in triumph. Joseph H. Choate, in his great oration on Rufus Choate, says of his kinsman: "From that rough pine cradle, which is still preserved in the room where he was born, to his premature grave at the age of fifty-nine, it was one long course of training and discipline of mind and character, without pause or rest." [10]

The testimony is therefore conclusive, though not absolutely, concerning the value of concentration. The following of a few departments of study creates greater and better power than the dissipation of intellectual forces. The "major" system, which most institutions in some form adopt, has much evidence in its favor. For instance, the four men from Johns Hopkins, who entered the Harvard Law School, and who took honors, in the twenty-six years between 1894 and 1920, pursued "major" courses, two in Latin and Greek, one in Mathematics, one in Physics, and one in Political Economy and History. The examination of the courses taken by the Yale graduates gives likewise conclusive evidence. Most students coming from Yale had devoted themselves to a few studies throughout their course. Seldom was a subject taken for a shorter period than two years, and not a few were pursued for three, or even for four. The reason for this consummate result is not far to seek. The scattering of the subjects of

[10] *The Life of Joseph Hodges Choate,* by Edward Sandford Martin, Vol. II, p. 57.

any general course means a study of the elements only of a subject. Concentration means the pursuing of the more advanced and difficult parts of a subject. It is such a pursuing which nourishes the mind. The need of such concentration is made the more emphatic and timely by the vast increase of the number of outside interests which command the student. These interests use up his time and consume his forces. "It seems too bad," said the late Thomas Day Seymour, of Yale, "to ask these men to study Greek. They have so many things to do!" Several of these interests, moreover, have a mighty intensity, and make a peculiarly forceful appeal to the undergraduate. Such increase of interests both in number and forcefulness is simply a transcript of the change in the mind and movement of the general community. It is, moreover, not to be forgotten that about one-half of the students are earning, at least, a part of their way through college. Such self-help, in many cases necessary—though not in all—represents a proportion of time and of a use of personal power which, if devoted to scholarly pursuits, would bring forth results far more adequate than janitor service or waiting on tables at the college commons can produce.

The interpretation of these facts also offers witness to the truth that, in certain cases, the college does not succeed in giving discipline or intellectual training to the student. The testimony is that a few students do not wake up in their college career, or at least do not wake up till near its ending. "He loafed; he was never known to study," is the testimony borne by an occasional report. It *is* borne, however, though seldom. Each teacher in an American college recognizes the condition. The typical student does not experience his intellectual conversion, his new birth—a change as real as are the physical changes of adolescence—until near the middle of his undergraduate career. Of course, in the law school, if not earlier, he does wake up and come to the consciousness that he is or has a mind.

As I have already intimated, the method of study is quite as important as, or more important than, the content. One question touching method relates to the pursuit of studies through the lecture or through the recitation system. The system of recitation is in America historically more common. The system of the lecture is a recent introduction. The chief differentiation is that the lecture gives information. The recitation gives opportunity for the close contact of mind with mind, for the intellectual wrestling of student with teacher, of teacher with student, of student with student. Recitation stands for collision, the lecture often for collusion. The recitation represents the Socratic method. It is the method of Mark Hopkins. It is the method of Henry Adams. The condition of a lecture class of one hundred or one thousand hearers forbids the use of this method. The lecture system represents the Demosthenic method; the recitation, as I have said, the Socratic. The lecture system, however much it may either inform or inspire, usually fails to promote the close, hard thinking which, as process and result, constitutes education.

The scholarly and pedagogical differences existing between colleges seem to play a large part in individual judgment and in public discussion regarding these colleges. These differences are in many minds strongly emphasized. The seven hundred reports and interpretations do not give support to such emphasis and differentiations. Of the more than six hundred colleges and universities recognized by the United States Commissioner of Education, about one-third may be properly regarded as of a high grade, at least of a grade high enough to warrant the Harvard Law School in receiving their graduates. I do not doubt that the differences dividing the institutions which form this group of one-third from those which form the larger group of two-thirds, are weighty, deep, fundamental. But the differences which separate the members of the smaller group from each other are far less fundamental and weighty in their educational value for the student than is usually believed. For, though certain outstanding institutions, noble in history, bearing long lists of graduates in which great names are fairly frequent, rich in endowment, amply provided with libraries and laboratories, including foremost scholars on their faculties, do seem to offer peculiarly rewarding advantages to their students, yet they are liable to be limited in their educational value by at least two considerations. First, they are prone to represent what may be called mass education. Their overflowing numbers almost forbid, or at least render difficult, the paying of just heed to the individual student. Second, the new student, by reason of such congestion, is prone not to devote himself to the doing of his intellectual duties. Not a few colleges, which are not historic, which are not rich in endowment, which are not well provided with books and scientific apparatus, are giving at least as good intellectual training for the study of the law, or indeed for the study of medicine or of divinity, to certain students, as is given by colleges historic and most outstanding. The differences, therefore, in the intellectual values of the education given by the better colleges are far less fundamental than is commonly believed.

A further remark also emerges. The number of honor men in the several classes has not increased as those classes themselves have increased. In the Class of 1880 in the Harvard Law School were twenty students; in the Class of 1881, thirteen; in the Class of 1882, twenty-four. In each of these classes there were, in 1880, six honor men; in 1881, eight honor men; in 1882, eleven honor men. Reviewing the three classes of the tenth decade of the nineteenth century: in the year 1891, of a class of forty-eight, seventeen were honor men; in 1896, of a class of one hundred and six men, seventeen won honors; in 1899, of a class of one hundred and twenty, twenty-one were honor men. In the first decades of the twentieth century, in 1901, there were one hundred and fifty-two graduates, of whom twenty-nine won honors; in 1906, two hundred graduates, of whom thirty-three were honor men; in 1909, one hundred and seventy-six, of whom seventeen won honors. Out of two hundred and eight in the Class of 1912, twenty-one received honors. In the Class of 1921, there were one hundred and seventy-five men, of whom sixteen won honors. It is, however, only fair to say of this last class that in and after the World War the work of students showed a certain disturbance and restiveness of mind which normally resulted in a diminution of men taking honors.

It is thus in general made clear that the number of honor men has not increased with the enlarging membership of the classes. This fact is impressive. The causes of the fact are not only impressive but possibly significant. The discovery of the causes offers a problem quickening to one's educational and human interest. Is the change caused by a hardening of the examinations for honors? In the opinion of certain members of the Harvard Faculty, it is not so caused. The examination papers of the Law School, for two score years, form an impressively consistent body of questions. Is the change caused by a stricter assessment of the answers themselves? The testimony is that the standards for assessing the questions have remained constant. Is the change caused by the transit in the undergraduate course from the severer to more general studies? This may certainly be a cause. Or does the cause lie in the diverse and diverting activities of undergraduates? This fact may represent the cause. The preceding paragraphs seem to give evidence for this conclusion. But clearly the evidence does not amount to proof, and perhaps proof is not to be sought in such atmospheric conditions. Is the change caused by the fact that so many men, and so many able men, too, are now going into business, who formerly would have gone into law? An affirmative answer seems to be not unreasonable. Is the change caused by a condition of less hard intellectual work on the part of the law students themselves? On the contrary, there is no evidence that the present law students are less laborious than their predecessors. Is the change caused by the fact that the conditions and methods now prevailing in the Harvard Law School are less effective in making scholars than those of the older time? Those who have the right to answer are inclined to say that the present conditions for teaching the third-year class of almost three hundred students, or the first-year class of almost four hundred, are not so promotive of scholarship as were the conditions of forty years ago for teaching classes of twenty men in the third, and of sixty men in the first, year. Is the change caused by a less efficient body of teachers? No professional school and no college has maintained for two score of years a better or more consistent level of noble instruction, given by men abler or more devoted. Forty years ago, the professors in the Harvard Law School numbered only five, but these five were Christopher Columbus Langdell, James Bradley Thayer, John Chipman Gray, Oliver Wendell Holmes, and James Barr Ames. There were also "instructors."

The number is now increased fivefold and more, and it is unnecessary to say that a very high order of excellence is still maintained. Is the change caused by the fact that the community has fewer able men who adopt the law as their calling? The population of the country has increased fast and vastly. In certain years, or for a period of a few years, certain colleges send to the Law School a body of specially brilliant graduates. For a time they continue, and then they cease to come. Why they come—this exceptionally able body—or why they cease to come seems to be as mysterious as why certain political leaders appear at an epoch and then vanish, leaving no successors. "The wind bloweth where it listeth." It may be that the present decade or quartette of years is a low tide in legal abilities.

A comprehensive induction, in conclusion, is to be drawn from these reports covering both the one hundred and four colleges and the Law School giving honors to these seven hundred and nine men. It is the inference that high honors won in the undergraduate career give promise of high honors to be won in the professional school. The large majority of these students were among the first, or were the first, scholars in their respective college classes. Prizes they constantly won. Membership in the Phi Beta Kappa was usually voted to them. Page after page of their reports offers evidence of their high scholarly standing. The places which these men held in the undergraduate college were prophetic of the places they held in the Law School; and, be it added, the places they held in the

Law School were a forecast of the places which they came to hold subsequently in their profession. The older men of the law classes of the early decades are now passing into the last years of their professional service. The men of the middle period are now in the midst of their professional career. Name after name found in the college and Law School lists represents the ablest lawyers at the bar and the wisest judges on the bench. Again it is found that intellectual ability is an enduring and consistent force, whatever may be the age of the men possessing it. It is as essentially true of first scholars and of the subsequently first citizens in the United States, to-day, as it was in the England of the early decades of the last century, as Macaulay said, that the honors men of Oxford and the tripos men of Cambridge make up a clear prophecy respecting the future leaders of government, of society, and of professional service.

X

AN AGE OF THE DISSIPATED MIND [1]

A DISSIPATED character is a dissolute character. It represents the man or woman who pursues pleasure as an aim or as a condition of life. It stands for wastefulness of personality. Not infrequently it represents wastefulness of money. It means the disintegration of life's strongest forces, unwisdom in the use of life's best powers, and degradation in the application of life's highest standards. A dissipated character represents indolence in work, coarseness in ethical texture, and is usually superficial and immediate in its selfish processes. The marks of the dissipated character help one to understand the dissipated mind.

A dissipated mind means a mind thin in knowledge and in thought. It has for its aim or condition immediate pleasure. Its breadth is superficial, its depth is slight, its height low, or if high, visionary and cloudy. It lacks working power. It has no method. Its logic is poetical, its philosophy without reasoning, its psychology of the rule of the thumb. It knows a bit about many things and not much of any. Its power of speech is in the inverse ratio of its power of reason-

[1] An address at the Founder's Day exercises of the Library School, Western Reserve University, June 15, 1922.

ing. Its speech flits from topic to topic like the butterfly, without the butterfly's beauty and grace. Its power of self-judgment results, usually, in a high degree of self-appreciation.

The causes of the dissipated mind are far more interesting than is the definition of the mind itself. Of these causes I name six.

The first cause is found in the drift of population from the country to the city. This condition seems very remote as a cause. But the connection is definite and strong. The fact of the drift of population from the country to the city is evident. The country stands for aloneness. Farms are separated each from the other. Life is solitary. Solitude leads to reflection. It promotes the contemplative mind. It nourishes meditation. Solitude, therefore, is the mother of mental processes which are individual. The process may be thin, but it is narrow. The process may be narrow, but it is personal. If personal, it is not dissolute or dissipated. The city, on the contrary, stands for the multitude. It means the crowd. It represents conformity. It recognizes the force of fashion. *A la mode* is its rule. Do what others do is its first and great commandment. Therefore, individuality in character is lost. The integrity of mind becomes dissipated.

A second cause lies in the variety and diversity of the subjects of education. This variety surpasses belief or possible understanding. It runs from mental training to manual training, from Greek to geography of all sorts, from dressmaking to metal trades, from ordinary writing and stenography to Latin and French. The cause of this vast variety in the curriculum is found in the variety and diversity of the life to which the school ministers. The cause leads to the result in the schools, and the result in the schools, in turn, emphasizes the variety and diversity of the life product. Contrast with the present conditions the schools of two generations ago. Few were the subjects, but these few were pursued with a thoroughness in method, with a length in time, now unknown. Education that is thorough in a few subjects tends to produce a mind that is strong, vigorous. Concentration creates definite power. Education in many and diverse subjects tends to produce the mind which, if alert, is thin in its content and superficial in its processes.

A third cause of the dissipated mind lies in that new force called the "movies." It is a good name. The force does move. Its soldiers always march with a double quick. Its automobiles run at one hundred and twenty miles an hour. Its heroines jump over cliffs quicker than half a wink. It is ever on the go. It trembles. It switches off and switches on, more often off than on. It delays not. It never stays. It appeals to the sensational. It allows no reasoning. Its promoters never have heard of the law of cause and effect. Its pictures appeal to the eye overstimulated, to the nerves overwrought, to the feelings overheated. Such a force, of course, dissipates the mind.

A fourth cause lies in the strain through which we, as a nation and as individuals, have been passing these last eight years. It has been, and still is, a strain, a strain on the whole man, a strain on the mind, the heart, the will. When one thinks that a ring of the telephone may mean a message of wounding or of dying on the French front, the exhaustion of the heart and of the nerve is constant and tremendous. The strain has also been the strain of important uncertainties and of uncertain importances. It has not been confined to war, however. It has touched business in all forms, and life in school and college. Of course, the mind, under this strain, becomes loose in its working, irritable in its relationships, captious in its conclusions.

The fifth cause lies in variety and diversity of interests, as represented in the daily newspaper. We are a people of the newspaper. We are, moreover, a people of headlines in the newspaper. We are a people not so much of the quarterly as of the monthly magazine, not so much of the monthly as of the weekly, not so much of the weekly as of the daily. In the daily, we are the people of the morning edition, of the evening edition, and, between the two, of the hourly edition. The daily paper represents a diversity of subjects as great as is the diversity of interests in life. These subjects are usually treated in a superficial way, in a way, too, in which events are unrelated to each other. Take any paper, the paper, for instance, which declares that it "prints all the news that is fit to print." I read the headlines—the *New York Times* of Saturday, June 3: "Poincare Upheld in Riotous Session," "Two Aviators Burned to Death in Texas Airplane Crash," "Strictures Rouse Harding to Wrath," "Negroes Kill and Wound Whites in Texas," "Phone Lines Cut as Armed Men Rushed to Scene," "Broadhurst Beaten After Row on Ship," "$5,500,000 Theatre for Times Square," "Cunningham Story Baffles Officials in Ward Mystery," "Will, Written in Verse, Gives All to the Wife," "Shows $20,000,000 Steel Merger Cash to 'Make a Market,'" "Proposes Inquiry on Harvard 'Ban,'" "Wants to Sell Husband's $25,000 Tomb to Relieve Poverty, Singer Tells Court." What is the condition of the mind brought up on such a pabulum? The ordinary reading of the daily newspaper by the ordinary mind cannot but result in intellectual dissipation. It does not represent reasoning. It is picturesque, but not logical. It is descriptive, but not interpretative. It is a series of facts, or supposed facts, but it does not represent relationship. It does not promote or discipline thinking.

The sixth and the last cause I name of the dissipated mind is that the forces of life, so great and diverse, are not ruled by great personalities. The social and other conditions are not obedient to commanding voices. In fact, there is no commanding voice. Ours is a democratic government. The world is becoming a democratic world. But democracy, adopting republicanism as its method, very easily passes over into Bolshevism. Democracy is liable to spell anarchy. Democratic law easily becomes lawlessness. It is a world in which, not only is each regarded as equal to every other, but in which each is held to be a little bit better than every other. Human chaos results. Our pictures are cubist pictures, in which the length and the breadth, the height and even the depth are equal. Our poetry is free verse. Our music is jazz. Moral outlawries obtain. Intellectual standards are broken. Dissoluteness in mind rules. Intellectual dissipation spreads out over the community like the freezing frost of December, or the hot winds of August.

XI

TO FIND THE SUPERIOR STUDENT[1]

ONE of the problems before the American college to-day is to find who are the superiors and who are the inferiors. If the college freshman is superior to the high-school senior, if the college sophomore is superior to the college freshman, so, it may be said, there are freshmen superior to other freshmen and sophomores superior to other sophomores.

The process begins at the college gateway. The testing of those who are able to pass that gateway, or who, having passed it, are able to continue within the academic quadrangles, is the great problem. For some fifteen years, the American college has been giving special tests, and for generations of years, more regular tests in the shape of formal examinations. At the present time, the colleges are using a dozen or so diverse types of methods for examining men and women for admission to the freshman class.

But the problem, as I have intimated, does not cease with the actual admission. The problem is to adopt methods which shall discover the superior student after he has become a college student. The problem is,

[1] Address at the Education Conference at Heidelberg University, at Tiffin, Ohio, June 20, 1925.

however, not a hard one. Turn it around; by what methods will you discover the inferior student? Alas, you need not search far or long. Inferior students uncover themselves. By parity of revelation or observation, superior students make themselves known. Remember the case of Burke and the horse shed. The wise teacher, knowing the intellectual point of view of his students, recognizing the power of learning, appreciating the power of interpretation, or of logical reasoning, acquainted with their diligences or their loafings, measuring their working power, acquainted with their physical health and psychological habits, finds it easy, and with a fair degree of accuracy, to discover, interpret, and to understand the superior man. Such were the methods used for the academic generations in Yale in determining the so-called "divisions" into which a student was put. Such were the methods employed at Harvard in the brief administration of the great Everett. They were abolished in the following term of President Sparks.

Many and diverse, however, are the yet more special means that are pursued in the various colleges. Perhaps Columbia represents the number and diversity of these methods quite as well as any college. They touch a discussion of such questions, or subjects, as these:

> Mercantilism was the result of the nationalistic commercial rivalry which has supplanted that of the Italian and German city-States;
>
> Voltaire admired experimental science and nat-

ural law, and was the ardent critic of contemporary conditions.

They represent also underlining certain words or phrases, in such statements as these:

> The followers of John Wesley are known as Quakers, Baptists, Methodists, Unitarians;
>
> Most of the inhabitants of the Baltic Isles belong to the race known as the Alpine, British, Teutonic, Mediterranean, Basque, Celtic.

The suggestions contained in these tests represent the comprehensiveness, the variety, of the examinations which all colleges are inclined to adopt. Measured in terms of ends, the methods are of tremendous worth.

The reasons for these new emphases on the fact of superior students, and on the methods for discovering them, are at least fourfold.

First. It is most obvious, gloriously and alarmingly obvious, that the number of students has become an academic flood. The increase, in the generation since 1890, is five hundred per cent. In this vastness, the increase of the ordinary or inferior class has, I am sure, been greater than five hundred per cent. The consequence is a sense of peculiar obligation to give proper heed to the superior.

With this fact is to be joined a second reason, namely, the inadequacy of the college to take proper care of the multitude. The inadequacy applies both to the teaching staff and to material facilities.

A third reason of the emphases lies in the increase

of the appreciation, on the part of the people, of the higher education. The value of the higher education in making a better living, and in making a life better worth living, has been vastly enhanced. The publication of the facts regarding the achievements in business or professional service of graduates has served to accentuate academic worths.

The fourth reason of the accentuated heed given to superior students is found in the increasing cost of the higher education. This cost is born of general, and of academic, conditions as well. It represents practically a doubling. It is, therefore, logical that so precious a force and asset should be devoted to the recipients who promise the largest returns for the enlarged investment.

In our discussion, the central and controlling question now emerges: What should be done for students of this higher type? Before making a specific answer, I wish to state a single, logical assumption or prolegomenon, namely, the atmosphere or environment for service to the superior student should be one of academic and personal freedom. This freedom is indeed to be exercised under supervision. That personal freedom, under which the Divine Author and Director of our being seems to place us, should find a duplicate in the last years of the college life of superior students. The conditions favor. For, visions and duties are contemporaneous, and each is commanding and supplementary. The teachings of the individual's past are heard, and they receive a more responsive heeding.

The prospects of the future are both alluring and prompting to service. The supervision of the college is watchful, but free from inquisitiveness. The older spectators on the shore watch the new academic seamen, as they launch forth into the deep, free to suggest, yet not free to suggest too much, and eager and able to give help in case of danger. Yes, the freedom of the superior student, under supervision, is, and should be, the prevailing atmosphere.

Yet, there are several direct methods of aiding, of which I shall note three.

The first is the devotion of the superior student to the great subjects. This devotion may lie in several methods. Courses of instruction are chief. Conferences with teachers are also commanding. The student's own reading or research, largely self-selected, has a great place. One's own writing, too, is not to suffer neglect. It is well for a student to choose a noble theme. Better to select a great field of study and of reflection of which only a partial mastery can be made, than a small one of which the mastery is less incomplete. The great theme calls out undiscovered forces. Indeed, it seems to create new powers. "As they went, they were healed." The large field, too, gives a vision of opportunity for study which may cover a whole lifetime. It represents concentration, and concentration tends to quicken consecration. The enclitics have their place and are good. But a book of Homer is better. Changes just introduced at Vassar give intimations of this method.

A second specific method of helping superior students lies in a somewhat opposing method, namely, the tutorial. This system takes on several forms. It is both historic and timely. But the essential element of each form is the bringing of the mind immature under the influence of the mind mature, of the mind superior under the influence of the mind more superior, of the mind learned under the influence of the mind more learned, of the mind responsive to inspiration and quickening under the influence of a mind yet more quickening and inspiring. Picture Plato beneath the plane trees with his students; think of Darwin and Henslow at Cambridge, of T. H. Green, of Jowett, of H. A. L. Fisher, at Oxford. What intimations of glorious reciprocities!

What I have just said intimates a third method, which, however, is a part of the second. It relates to the worth of the great individual person, the teacher, to the great individual person, the student. To this form, the college needs to give itself. Great scholars in teachers' chairs are good. Great teachers in teachers' chairs are better. Great characters, who are also great teachers, are best, supremely best. For achieving this end, no rewards are too rich, no stipends too high, no appreciations too hearty.

In the choice of teachers who are, or who have, great character, the college should exercise more care, more constant diligence. One of the last and more precious of the noble works which Burton did in, for and through the University of Michigan lay in promoting certain standards for selecting members of the teaching staff. But, however full, definite, and high these standards may be made, it is yet to be remembered that in the application of these standards—and Burton would be one of the first to recognize the truth—the element of personal greatness has primary worth. Herein the older college, the college of Mark Hopkins, of Albert Hopkins, of John Bascom, of Perry, the college of William G. Sumner, and the college of Diman, had a priceless worth.

It is also to be said that herein, too, the small, as well as the older, college has a field of infinite depth and of infinite worth. The large college gives education to masses, and it is good. The small college gives personal education, and it is better. The large college is prone to be concerned with means, and it is well. The small college is concerned with methods, which is yet better. The large college is prone to be taken up with mechanics, with machines, and with mechanisms, which are necessary. The small college is concerned with the essential and inherent substance of education, with the person, which is better and which is best. The large college represents the factory system, the small the spinning wheel and the hand loom.

The perils and the advantages of any system of caring for the superior student are to be specially weighed.

For, of course, perils there are. Of the perils, I wish to mention and to give brief comment upon three. The first relates to the ordinary student, and the second to the superior one. After all, the ordinary student represents the normal field and force of the ordinary college. To change Lincoln's remark, "God must like ordinary students, for he has made so many of them." We must like them, too. We are to labor for them, to think for them, to confer with them, to inspire them on their laborious way. Our privileges with the few superiors should not, and I am sure do not, lessen our sense of duty toward the common ones.

A second peril concerns the superior student himself. For he is to be saved from himself. He needs to be saved, for his abilities may easily become disabilities. His superiorities are prone to gravitate downward into inferiorities. His power offers a temptation to cockiness, to self-esteem, to pride, to glorying which is vanity. From such unhappiness for himself and for others, he is to be saved. He is to be kept humble by measuring himself against the highest standards, and he is to maintain a proper self-esteem by recognizing that power ever creates obligation. That the greatest are ever the humblest, on the American college campus to-day, is quite as true as it was on the "backs" at Cambridge in Newton's time.

A third peril lies in the fact that, while seeking to train superior minds, there may occur a neglect of the one great intellectual force, that force which may be called the national mind. Of the national mind, Josiah Royce—whose too early death still quickens keenest regret—said:

> That traditional college has as its chosen office the training of individual minds. The modern

> university has as its highest business, to which all else is subordinate, the organization and advance of learning. Not that the individual minds are now neglected. They are wisely regarded as the servants of the one great cause. But the real mind which the university has to train is the mind of the nation, that concrete social mind whereof we are all ministers and instruments. The daily business of the university is, therefore, first of all, the creation and the advance of learning, as the means whereby the national mind can be trained.

This interpretation of Royce was made in the year 1891, and it still has great truth. Yet, the interpretation may, in part at least, be answered to the effect that a method of training the national mind is to train the superior minds of individual students. To get national leading, one needs first to get individual light. To get scholarly forcefulness for the whole community, one needs to achieve and to quicken the scholarly forcefulness of the minds of individuals.

Yet the advantages and worths of devoting peculiar heed to superior students are far more weighty than are the perils. Of these advantages I venture to specify four.

One of the advantages lies in the fact that the emphasis of the college education is thus placed on concerns intellectual. The college to-day is beset by at least two dangers. The first that I name is the danger of the substitution of the stadium for the studium. It is the danger of athleticism. We all recognize the peril. Every college faculty deplores it. The thoughtful in the community mourn over it. It is felt in the responsiveness of the student body to sports. It is heard in the tumults and the shouting of the bleachers. It is seen in the pages of reports given to football games. As I read these reports, in headlines or paragraphs, it all seems to me to be a sort of bullfight, made for the thrilling of spectators who have paid their dollar or more for their thrills. The college is also, contrariwise, beset by the peril of laziness on the part of students. This student is not a superior student. College idleness is made a business. Loafing is a profession. What should be an avocation, the by-process and the by-products of the campus, has become a vocation, and what should be a vocation, hard mental work, has become an avocation. "Activities" have taken the place of activity. From these two perils, the giving of heed to the superior students is a safeguard. This heed acts as a high dam to hold back the athletic stream, and also lays deep-down, rock-bed foundations to resist the insidious forces of idleness. The great ends are thus accentuated. The college is made still to stand for *veritas.* Its flag bears the symbol, *lux.* Thus are discovered such philologists as Joseph Wright of Oxford, professor of Comparative Philology, born in a Yorkshire cottage of one room, at the age of six working for thirty cents a week, teaching himself to read at the age of thirteen, and, in the next seven years, teaching himself Latin, Greek, French, and German, who came to be a master of many languages and literatures and in 1901 succeeded Max Müller in a noble Oxford professorship. The method also helps to discover great scientists, such as Pupin, for instance, who, landing in New York with five cents in his pocket, has added millions upon millions of dollars to the worths of the world, and has become one of the tremendous causes of adding to the happiness of countless millions of people.

A second advantage lies in the comfort which this method gives to benefactors. The American college of private foundation appeals with constant urgency, or with urgent constancy, to the American public for endowment. Not a few of those who give, give, as was the custom of the first years of Harvard and Yale, out of hard-earned money, out of small savings, out of poverty. Such givers still abound. Such givers are, to-day, asking themselves the question, "Why should I give of my economies to support institutions which are seemingly devoted to the training of athletes and to the promotion of idleness of young gentlemen?" Inevitable questions are these. Care given for superior students assures such conscientious supporters that their offerings are devoted to the high purposes of the higher education.

A third advantage also emerges. Such care for the superior student gives a rich blessing to the superior teacher. Such care and interest quicken his routines unto varieties, verities, and vitalities. Such care and interest reënforce his teaching unto keen alertness. Such solicitude serves to deepen the belief that one great value of truth lies in truthfulness; truth becomes thus transmuted through personal application. Agassiz declared that the greatest result of his work in America was his discovery and training of three men.

This advantage leads me to the fourth worth of such care for superior students. It is the last which I shall name, namely, the college thus aids in the promotion of the noblest life of America and of the world. It thus helps to build civilization. It thus seeks to eliminate blind, hard force and to bring in an age of noble thinking, pure feeling, and rich achieving. It thus does its bit toward the founding of the Divine Kingdom, of which Isaiah prophesied, and Virgil sang in the fourth Eclogue. It thus seeks to lift the human mountains unto even higher heights. From these hilltops flow streams to gladden the prairie levels of the communal and of the academic world.

XII

ACADEMIC EQUIVALENTS IN PEACE TIME FOR WAR [1]

ONE year ago to-day I spoke to you on the duties of the soldier-student. Among these duties I named obedience, full devotion to a single cause, coöperation, and a broad-minded and broad-hearted patriotism. The war has ended. The S.A.T.C. has disbanded. Yet the great qualities named one year ago as duties of the soldier-students have value also to you. Other qualities there are, too, which have value in times of peace.

The question, therefore, which I wish to discuss to-day is the question of finding an equivalent in peace time for the results which obedience, devotion, coöperation, and patriotism brought to the student in war time.

And, first, let me say, in preparation for what may follow, that education should be like war in at least one fundamental element. It should be democratic. War makes equals. It promotes equality between men of the same grade or kind. If it creates differences and distinctions between different grades of service, it yet makes men of the same order equal. All privates

[1] Address given to the students of Western Reserve University at the beginning of the academic year, September 23, 1919.

in the ranks are alike. Exterior distinctions are dropped. The titled are as obscure as the obscure; the obscure as distinguished as the titled. The poor are as rich as the rich and the rich are as poor as the poor. A boy of distinguished ancestry and education, brought up in peculiarly exclusive surroundings, was serving at the front as a private. In a letter to his mother he told about two of his special chums. One of them was named Erine O'Callahan and the other Billie Sweeney. He wrote to his mother: "You can't beat those boys on the face of the earth. I want you to call upon their mothers." Real education is likewise democratic education—a common obedience for all men, themselves equal or unequal; an equality of opportunity. It has been said that in Germany there are no equals, only superiors or inferiors. In America one might, with equal truth, say there are only equals. America holds open one educational gateway. It paves one road to learning, and that not royal. It points out one goal which it inspires each to reach. Aristocracy in education is narrow and narrowing, inclined to accept social stratification. Democracy in education is broad, as broad as human nature. Aristocracy in education is prone to be materialistic. Democracy is idealistic. Aristocracy in education is liable to forget humanity's hard, complex problems. Democracy in education is sympathizing with and inspiring to every worthy endeavor.

On this basis of democracy, therefore, the student should find an equivalent to war in certain elements or qualities of the college. Of these qualities I want to speak.

The first is to make hard work orderly and necessary. The life of the soldier is arduous. Every hour has its task, every condition its duty. The soldier is under orders. His day begins early, and taps find him eager to turn in. Each day is full in and of itself, and each day is a preparation for to-morrow. Every duty is his emergency; he is to be in readiness. The hospital or the guardhouse is the answer to the petition to be excused. The charge is constantly and forcefully made against the college student that he is not a hard worker, that he is not prepared for duty, that he is careless in manner, slothful and disorderly in intellectual habits, and that he is not quick and alive for an instant call to service. Fathers sometimes say to me: "I am not sending my boy to college, for he will come home lazy and self-indulgent. I want to get him an appointment at West Point where he cannot shirk." Therefore, I affirm to you that an equivalent for the training of the camp is hard, intellectual work on the campus. Read your lessons? Yes, and much. Study your lessons? Yes, and more. Think your lessons? Yes, and most. Be a hard taskmaster to yourself, harder than any one might have the right to be to you. Time is the only thing you have. Therefore, proportion your time wisely. Be a good fellow, by all means. Do not purchase time and the chance for study at the cost of good-fellowship. Do not be sullen and contemptuous. You need not be. You can be a gentleman and a student, a good fellow and a thinker, a friend and a hard reader. Endure hardship as a good student.

Through such hard work you will create for yourself two primary values in life. One of them I call resources. You will have as a result a not unworthy intellectual bank account. You will not find your drafts returned to you marked "O.D." Behind the Niagara Falls of your doing there must be the Great Lakes of thinking and of knowledge. Lake Superior is necessary for the Niagara River. The second result which hard work will give to you is a result alluded to in an address which Field Marshal Sir Douglas Haig made on being presented with the freedom of the city of London. It is the result called character. Sir Douglas is reported to have said: "We should not forget that the highest aim of education is not the attainment of certain limited commercial qualifications, but the formation of character, and the acquirement of that habit of mind which, alike in manhood as in boyhood, is always at school and has never done with learning."

A second element of college life equivalent to the training of war is the element of discipline. By discipline I mean respect for the rules of the college. The rules of this and of most colleges are few and rather general. They are laid down somewhat like rails on a stairway on the pier—to keep one from falling down or going over. They are designed to lessen risk. One can possibly evade them. Students often succeed for a time in escaping the penalty for breaking them. But such attempts are foolishness; in fact, these rules should be needless. Good swimmers do not need life preservers. Your own personal discipline should be so hard, so close, so constant, that the fact of the college discipline should never occur to you. The strong man as he walks gives no thought to the laws of equilibrium; he has learned to steady himself. Hold yourself down to the college law till you have mastered the rules, and then you will have found your power, and in power—freedom. We say constantly that the discipline of the school has become loose, that the discipline of the courts and the requirement of the law is distinguished by its breaches. But let the discipline of the college be firm, orderly, inevitable. Accept it. Profit by it. Let the discipline you give yourself in these college years be even firmer, more orderly, more inevitable, becoming like the procedure of the military court and camp.

There is a third element which may be found as an equivalent to the life and work of war. It is perhaps the most important of all. It is difficult to find the right name for it. I might call it patriotism or unselfishness, or the sense of humanity. I might possibly call it imagination. At any rate, imagination is the method or the intellectual way in which it makes its appeal. It is the human emotion created by the imagination. It is that sense that one is living a great life, doing a great work, inspired by a great motive, measuring up to the greatest possibilities within one's bounds. It is keeping step with one's fellow soldiers in life's march. It is the sense of music in one's soul. It is the meaning of the lump in the throat. On the college campus in the humdrum of the day, in the staid process of the unvarying weeks, how can one get and keep this high type of human patriotism and of unselfishness, of glorious devotion? How can one keep one's self responsive to life's thrills? How can one hold the music in one's soul? How can one retain the sense of the far-off, heavenly vision?

Yet, let me before answering add that it is unsafe for you to seek to live constantly on the highest levels, like people eight thousand feet above the sea level. You may not be able to breathe. The strings of the violin do not last if they are always screwed up tight to concert pitch. Yet, you cannot afford not to keep your mind upon a high plateau. How can you thus live?

In answer, let me say, and briefly, first: think in great terms and on great themes. Second: read a piece of literature every day. Third: know and feel as fully as you can the significance of the historic movements of your own time, movements perhaps the most significant of all history. Fourth: interpret history and science in their large relations. Fifth: apply to yourself, and closely, all these interpretations which you make. Sixth: sacrifice constantly the lower to the higher, and let the lower be worthy and the higher more worthy. Seventh: love the best.

College boys and other boys won the war. Some laid down their lives, and all were willing to. It were a tragedy indeed, and truly more tragic than their graves in Flanders' fields, if you should prove recreant to your duty, to your duty in peace and in the home of Alma Mater. Their service and their sacrifice without you will not be made perfect. Therefore, I declare the ninety-third year of this ancient college to be begun, and I pray for the blessing of the eternal God of wisdom to rest upon it in giving you strength to make it worthy of a good past and preparative of a yet better future.

XIII

RELATION OF THE LEGAL PROFESSION TO A LIBERAL EDUCATION[1]

WHAT are the needs of America which the lawyer, possessed of a liberal education, can most adequately fill? The two most significant phrases in the question are the lawyer and liberal education. In answer, I might speak negatively, telling what these needs are not. I must, however, be content with speaking positively, interpreting what these needs are that can thus be more and most fully met.

The community needs to save its institutions. The community, in its essential elements, rests down upon five institutions. They are the civil government, the school, the church, the family, and the institution of property. These are the bulwarks of the commonwealth. At present, these institutions are beset by perils. Government is beset by blocks, by the group system, by immediate executive action as a substitute for law, on the one side, and on the other, by the superfluity of laws. The school is beset by vocational narrowness and indifference to higher learning and teaching. The church is beset by the loss of its sacred day, by doubt

[1] Address delivered before the New York County Lawyers' Association, New York, Hotel Astor, evening of February 28, 1925.

of the authority of its sacred books, by heresy toward its creed, and by a mild contempt for its priesthood. The family is beset by easy divorce and by the disintegrating forces of which easy divorce is the token. Individual property is beset both by socialism and by communism. In general, the sense of historic continuity is dulled. Traditions are flung to the breezes of thoughtless indifference, or torn by the tempests of Bolshevik hatred. The community forgets the determinative unity of the past with the present, and of the present with the future. Social experimentation is the constant demand. The political constitution is in peril of being made a by-law, or a by-word, which one is to "get by." The common law is outlawed, and the statute is recognized as a point either of departure or of defiance or of disobedience. In the community is found a unique combination of indifference and of intolerance—of indifference to all except to one's own immediate concerns; of intolerance to personal or partisan antagonisms. Speed takes the place of considerateness; superfluity of thoroughness; the external of the vital; things of personality; showiness of reality; bigness of excellence; absorption in the immediate in time and space of a noble idealism and of far-flung highest aspirations. The principles of this interpretation are found in a copy of the morning's papers. I quote certain headlines of the first page of a leading New York paper of the morning of my writing: "Asserts Admiral Edited Out Truth of Warship Bombing," "All Taxis Halted as 5,000 Policemen Question Drivers," "Soldier Murdered Buried by Slayer," "Columbia Girl Shot by an Insane Friend in Her Hotel Room," "Police in New Drive to Clean Up Stage," "Newly Bulgarian Envoy Assassinated."

The needs of the individual, too, are not unlike the needs of the community. In particular, the individual lacks a sense of reasoned truthfulness. Truth, important as it is, is less important than truthfulness. For, truth is concerned, primarily, with the single fact. Truthfulness represents the proper relations of facts. To these proper relations is to be added a moral implication. The proper relations of facts as the results of observation and of reasoning, which one may know and enjoy, are precious. Reasoning is most precious. In this reasoning is found a need of the use of a sense of proportional evaluations, giving a just appreciation of methods, conditions, ultimate ends. The individual also stands in need of intellectual altruism. His mental eye is turned too constantly in upon itself. He therefore is half blind. He fails to understand the conditions of his brother. He fails to appreciate evidences touching the other man. Or, if he sees these evidences, he fails to weigh them or to declare the resulting conclusions. His mood and mode are liable to be an intellectual glaucoma. With this intellectual unresponsiveness, however, is joined a keen and forceful executive leadership. This leadership, though blind, is progressive. The individual goes, and is determined to go, though scarce knowing the goal of the journey. In some way he is sure he will muddle through. In this mood there is present a lack of personal humility. Chauvinism too easily abides in his soul and rests on his shoulders.

There is a third need of the community to which I must refer, even if briefly. The community needs a baptism of idealism. It needs to see visions and to dream dreams. It is absorbed in the practical and the material. It devotes itself to the immediate, the timely, the present. It looks down into the earth. It fails to see the stars. It clothes itself in purple and fine linen. It surrounds itself with luxuries. It glories in the senses. The senses become the sensual. The sensual easily passes over into the sensational, and the sensational, if continued, becomes the senile, even while the years are few and young. The community needs a sense of the eternal values, of the infinite worths. It needs the vision of faith. It hears the gospel of Schopenhauer and Nietzsche, and is deaf to Plato and Isaiah.

Now turns my little talk. What can the lawyer of a liberal education do to improve these conditions, to correct these evils, to guide the community unto a goal worthy of its origin and of its circumstance, and to give worthy support to the institutions of the social and civil order?

The lawyer of liberal education is adequately trained, more adequately trained than the members of other professions, to meet these needs of the nation and of the nations. For, the college stands for truth, for reasoned truth, for reasoned truthfulness. The most common word upon the shield of the college of America, or of the world, is the word *lux.* Often united with this word, as in the shield of Yale University, is the word *veritas.* The student's training represents a learning of the truth, and a reasoning about the truth which is learned. His education represents what Henry Adams used to call, as being the essence of education, "the weighing of evidence." His profession represents the weighing of evidence. The college student gains a preparation for its steady and constant practice. The college represents proportional evaluations—the less as less, the least as least, the much as much, and the most as most. Such evaluations represent analysis: the separation of a complex condition, of manifold forces, and diverse elements. A liberal education also stands for synthesis—a more difficult process than analysis—the putting together, into large judgments, of related parts. It stands for intellectual altruism. It means the entering into other men's minds, seeing with their mental eyes, understanding their principles, appreciating their prejudices, sympathizing with their conditions and circumstances, appreciating their methods, anticipating their purposes. Liberal education represents conciliation in fact, and conciliatoriness in mood. The profession of the law is one of collisions resulting in conciliations. The lawyer needs, therefore, to appreciate the intellectual mood and to understand the executive mode of his opponent. The profession stands for intellectual and intelligent guidance as more important than executive action. It accepts personality as more essential than the material, the vital as more precious than things. It aids in sober and adequate use of our complex English speech, both as cause and result of sober and accurate thinking. The lawyer, therefore, of liberal education, thus endowed, is able to serve the community with intelligence, with directness of method, with largeness of vision, unto the realization of highest aims.

Such services, as I thus seek to interpret them as belonging to the individual in relations to other individuals, belong still more to him in his relationship to the whole community. The lawyer of liberal education makes the richest offerings for the upholding of the five primary institutions of society. To the civil government, he gives constitution and statute, and the interpretation of both statute and the constitution. The lawyer usually makes the law. In such a service he is the guardian of that primary condition and primary right, civil liberty. In an address, given in the Inner Temple Hall, in the year 1908, on "The English Bar," Mr. Asquith said:

> Gentlemen, I make this claim, that there is no class or profession in our community which has done more—I will go further, I will say that there is none which has done as much—to define, to develop, and to defend the liberties of England. Sir Thomas More, Lord Coke himself, Selden, Somers, Camden, Romilly—those are but a few of the names selected almost at random from a long and illustrious roll. They were all bred in

> the common law of England, which is not a compendium of mechanical rules written in fixed and indelible characters, but a living organism, which has grown and moved in response to the larger and fuller development of the nation. The common law of England has been, still is, and will continue to be, both here and wherever English communities are found, at once the organ and the safeguard of English justice and English freedom.[2]

To the church, also, the lawyer ministers, in the maintenance of its rights. Witness the present Andover-Harvard litigation in the Supreme Court of Massachusetts. To the school, he ministers in obliging the community to educate its youth unto understanding. To the family he ministers in adding to the religious sanctities of that primary foundation the sanction of the law, as witnessed in the institution of marriage. Underlying each of the four institutions, of government, of the school, of the church, of the family, he seeks to maintain the integrity of property, as an individual or corporate right. In the common law and the statute, in the probate and other courts of the Commonwealth, he finds his instruments. In the threat of socialism or of communism, he stands as a warrior, armed to beat down the enemies of the State and of the individual. He—this man, bred in the historic college—is the upholder of the historic continuities of the people. He is the preserver of traditions, social and governmental.

[2] *Occasional Addresses: The English Bar,* by the Right Hon. H. H. Asquith, p. 121.

He recognizes that there was a yesterday, and that to-day is made richer by its bequests. He knows that, if some of the keys of the past are "blood-rusted," yet they are keys and can be used to unlock the doors of the present and of the future. If he is, at times, a radical, to remove the evils of the present and to prevent the evils of the future, he is also a conservative, to gather up and to preserve the good and the goods of a long and self-sacrificing past. If his vision, in time far-flung, is full, in space it is also large. He, this broadly trained mind, recognizes and uses government "by the people and for the people," a democratic government by and through republican methods. He is the foe of government by groups. For, government by groups is group government. The college, which is a community, has educated him unto great communal concerns, by sympathetic methods, through enlarged forces, under general conditions. He, this liberally trained man, does not believe in the liberty of equality or the fraternity of the mob which burns and murders, but in the freedom of the stars in a social and civil firmament in which each pursues its orbit without jar or hindrance, in a well-ordered and beneficent world.

The college also aids the liberally educated lawyer to maintain the idealism which is a need of the community. For, the college prolongs the period of youth which is the age of ideals. The college nourishes friendships which are at once the soil and the soul of idealism. The college gives quickening to self-sacrifice, and forgetfulness of selfish forms and forces. The college gives to life imagination, poetry, vision. Through many forces does the college make this richest contribution toward the maintenance of idealism. One form of this manifold force relates to the teacher. How great is the debt you graduates of Amherst owe to Garman, that philosophic, self-sacrificing soul! How lasting is the obligation which you graduates of Yale feel toward Hadley and toward Sumner of the earlier time! How full of love are your hearts, you graduates of Harvard, to the wise Palmer, the suggestive James! Your profession practices, as well as your lives bear evidence to, and proof of, the worth of those who helped to give you a liberal education. They have helped you to achieve. They have helped to transmute your life into a poem. The liberal education has given to you a sky.

The lawyer, this man of trained power, has an endowment of heart, cultured, quite as rich as of mind, disciplined. He is both to think truly and to feel rightly. His service to the individual or to the community gives a field for his emotional, as well as for his intellectual, forces. He appreciates that it is a moral obligation to be intelligent. He recognizes the worth of ideals, which are ideas made the object of attainment. He knows that ideals are forces which determine the realities of life. He knows that on the cardinal virtues swing the weighty and silently moving doors of character, doors opening into an infinite universe. He appreciates the value of excellence and worth, which the American democracy, governmental and communal, is prone to depreciate. For mere bigness, he has a smile, if not a blow, knowing that the winds which have enlarged it will presently cause it to shrink. He, this man of the college classroom, has, in his soul and in his bearing, the promotion also of tolerance. For, he has learned a bit how cubical is truth, how broad and how diverse are the needs of the community, how individual are the wants of the citizen, and how high are the aspirations of our God-created humanity. He yet feels the unity of the race and the races. For, he has not forgotten the teaching of the college pulpit, that of one blood are made all nations of men. He, in his intellectual vision, is taught that moral convictions are more important than inductions, and that moral convictions are the ruling forces for the government of States, and for the betterment of men.

Likewise, in method and circumstance, for the individual and for the community, this lawyer, college-bred, incarnates the noblest forces. If speed is a besetting sin or method of American procedure, he is willing still to take time—some say, too willing to take too much time. For, he recalls Burke's remark, that States move slowly. He is our noblest savior from panics political, which are as menacing as are panics financial. If superficiality is also a besetting sin of our conditions, he is trained unto a sense of deep relationships. In one he seems much and many. If radicalism is our atmosphere, he seeks to transmute that atmosphere into forces for the permanence of the State, through noblest thinking, and through present and highest feeling. He thus endeavors to bring in the age which shall be golden without being the age of gold.

If one were to seek for examples, among your own members, of a lawyer of such a type, one could easily call up great names. The names of Evarts and of Carter readily spring to the lips. I content myself, however, with repeating what Joseph H. Choate once said to the bench and bar of England at Lincoln's Inn, a score of years ago, in a farewell address·

> Until I became an Ambassador and entered the *terra incognita* of diplomacy I believed a man could be of greater service to his country and his race in the foremost ranks of the Bar than anywhere else; and I think so still. To be a priest, and possibly a high priest, in the temple of justice, to serve at her altar and aid in her administration, to maintain and defend those inalienable rights of life, liberty, and property upon which the safety of society depends, to succor the oppressed and to defend the innocent, to maintain Constitutional rights against all violations, whether by the Executive, by the Legislature, by the resistless power of the Press, or, worst of all, by the ruthless rapacity of an unbridled majority, to rescue the scapegoat and restore him to his proper place in the world—all this seemed to me to furnish a field worthy of any man's ambition.[3]

[3] *The Life of Joseph Hodges Choate,* by Edward Sandford Martin, Vol. II, p. 283.

But I presume Mr. Choate might have added, if the occasion allowed, as I do venture now to add, that these highest functions could be best performed, best for the individual and for the community, by one possessed of liberal learning and by one to whom and in whom a liberal learning had come to its full and ripe fruitage of disciplined power.

Such are some of the deepest needs of American life which the lawyer, who is liberally educated, is nobly and adequately fitted to meet.

XIV

MEDICAL ETHICS[1]

> LYDGATE'S hair never became white. He died when he was only fifty, leaving his wife and children provided for by a heavy insurance on his life. He had gained an excellent practice, alternating, according to the season, between London and a Continental bathing place; having written a treatise on gout, a disease which has a great deal of wealth on its side. His skill was relied on by many paying patients, but he always regarded himself as a failure: he had not done what he had once meant to do.

Thus George Eliot writes of a doctor in the last chapter of *Middlemarch.* It is to aid you a bit, if perchance I am able, in doing what you "mean to do," that I am here to-night: to aid you not in the attainment of technical knowledge or securing discipline in the art of healing, for these purposes you have other and competent instructors; but rather I am here to suggest some ethical or moral relations of which you are a part. These relations you already anticipate. They belong to you quite as much as human beings

[1] A lecture delivered before the students of the Medical Department of Western Reserve University.

as they belong to you as physicians. What is called medical ethics is simply ethics applied to the work of the doctor: it is essentially the universal law of right which belongs to the lawyer, mechanic, merchant, everyman. This profession of medicine finds its need in disobedience to this law. The minister is concerned with man in relation to obedience to the law of God; the lawyer is concerned with man in relation to obedience to the law of man; the doctor is concerned with man in relation to the laws of nature, which are none the less laws of God. If man had not broken the laws of God, the minister would not be needed; if man had not broken the laws of man, the bench and bar would be superfluous; if man had not broken the laws of his nature, the physician would be needless, however charming. We call breaking God's law a sin, breaking the statute a crime; wilfully breaking the laws of one's being is both a sin and a crime, for one's being has at once divine and social relations. The doctor has for his purpose to mend broken laws. The man is sick because he or some one has broken a law; the doctor is called to repair the ravages.

A profession differs from a trade in that, in the trade the relation between the seller and the buyer is commercial. In a profession the relation between the giver and receiver is personal. In a trade, money is the aim avowed and represents the method pursued. In a profession, money is neither the aim nor the method, only a condition. You are members of a profession; your purpose is not pecuniary; your purpose is humanitarian, philanthropic. To gain wealth should be no motive to the doctor. Having this motive, you cannot be a worthy physician, any more than a minister, with a like motive, can be a worthy minister. If to gain wealth be a purpose of the physician, his motives are at once unprofessional and unmoral. The presence of this motive in any degree vitiates the best work of the doctor, and him it degrades.

No class of professional men is more unselfish than the medical. The true doctor never spares himself. Like Paul, he is in watchings and fastings, in weariness and fatigue, in hunger and thirst, in journeyings often, in death oft, in perils in the city, in perils in the wilderness, in perils among false brethren; but all these dangers and hardships he endures. His endurance constitutes his glory. His reward is as much richer than gold as faith is better than cash. " 'Tis not the grapes of Canaan that repay, but the high faith that failed not by the way." Of the rich doctor one entertains just suspicion, even if he have great professional skill and honorable practice. Wealth not associated with professional skill points to quackery. The doctor is not to look upon his patient through a legendary mist of gold. He should rather see his patient in the light of truth. He is to see his patient as He who is called the Great Physician, Jesus, would see him—a man needing help, and a help which he himself can offer. I do not mean that the doctor is unworthy of his fees, but I do mean to say that the doctor shall not think of his fees more than Agassiz thought of money, and I do also mean that the doctor should think of his fees as Agassiz thought of money—as a necessary means of carrying forward his work. Thus freed from pecuniary motives, the doctor goes to his patient with clearness of penetration, with calmness of temperament, and with healthfulness of his entire nature, such as he is able to have and to cultivate. Though he does not believe in the mind cure, he recognizes the fact that seldom is the body diseased but that the mind or the mind's organ in the body is sympathetic—such a unit is man. He also, therefore, recognizes that his own mind is to be clear, vigorous, comprehensive, healthy, healthful. If he does not believe in the faith cure, he does believe in the value of hope as a curative agent, and also he believes that the faith of the patient in him as a doctor is ever to be fostered. He also knows that his own faith promotes faithfulness. He knows that a conscience calloused as horn, or misguided by false evidence, or outraged by disobedience, is often the cause, and, in some cases, the result of physical sickness. His own conscience, therefore, is ever to be kept as sensitive as his eyeball, as correct in its interpretations as reason can make it, and as obedient to the categorical imperative as God himself. He knows that a diseased motive is often the cause, sometimes the result, of a diseased body; he, therefore, as a physician, knows the duty of having his body controlled by a right motive. He is to have a sympathy which shall be as unlike the sympathy which a veterinary surgeon has for a dog with a broken leg, as it shall be unlike the sympathy which a mother has with her baby in diphtheria. He is to be neither a piece of steel nor a weeping Niobe. He is to be a gentleman, for he is to be with gentlemen and ladies. He is not to forget, either, that he is to be a gentleman when he is among those who are not gentlemen or ladies. He is to remember also as he enters the sick room, that, though he is a gentleman, he is simply a physician. His will he may suffer to bend to his patient's wish, but his will is never to be broken. Every appetite is to lie bound silent and at the foot of perfect self-control. He is to have patience in his willingness to suffer, and patience also in the persistence of his endeavor. He is to be truthful. He may not be obliged always to tell the whole truth, but he is never to tell an untruth. The occasions when a doctor believes it is necessary to tell an untruth are few, very few. Discrimination can always avoid revelations which may work ill. A man is very sick. The doctor sincerely fears that he cannot get well. The sick man asks the doctor: "Do you think, doctor, I shall get well?" What shall be the doctor's reply? He may say, "Sir, I think you will die," an answer as needless as it is cruel, and promotive of the very end which the doctor is trying to avoid. Such an answer is inexcusable. To such a question, an answer fair to the patient and just to the one answering should invariably be made. Is not this such a reply? "My dear friend, you are a sick man. You are very sick, but men sicker than you have recovered. You do your best; I will do my best; we will both work together in good hope." Thus a minister of courage and of hope is the doctor to be. He is not to shrink or to shirk. As writes one doctor:

> In no vocation are hope, assurance, sympathy, in fact, every quality that makes helpful man, more needed than here, for all sorts and conditions of men and women (many most revolting) appeal to us, and only that their need is so great can they be approached with the tenderness that will treat all men as brothers, all women as sisters. The temptation is great to persistently seek the agreeable and evade the disagreeable.

It is, I think, because of the power of temptation to seek the agreeable and to evade the disagreeable that many doctors are led into the excessive recommendation of opiates and stimulants. Doctors shrink from seeing a man suffer pain, however caused; it is painful to the witness as well as to the sufferer. A few grains of opium in some one of the many forms of preparation and of application give release from pain. So also the recommendation of alcoholic liquors may form a bridge which feeble feet may walk easily for a time and be released from the necessity of climbing the steep precipices leading to health. But the physician should not be influenced unduly by the desire to stop pain. It is easy to stop pain. The guillotine does it. The graveyard has no sufferers. The purpose of the doctor, I wish to say, is not to stop pain, but it is to promote health. In such promotion, in curing the special sickness, he is to have exceeding care that his curing of this sickness should not entail results which are more disastrous than this sickness itself. Each one of you can recall instances in which, through either ignorance or carelessness or misjudgment, the doctor has brought a withering blight upon human life by the use of alcoholic or other stimulants.

Therefore, in relation to your patient, let me say comprehensively, do not carry a long face into the sick room, do not be funereal; do not carry a broad face into the sick-room, do not be flippant; do not gossip, do not tattle; do not talk about yourself, do not talk about other patients; do not pretend to know everything, do not be ignorant of anything which, by studying, you can learn; do not make your patient sicker by staying too long; do not make him think he is not geting his money's worth by staying too short; do not fall in love with your women patients—it is bad manners and there is small danger—do not let them fall in love with you—of this there is less danger; do not come to the bedside with your clothing reeking with tobacco or with cologne; do not try any more experiments than are needful; do not fuss; do not complain; be a man.

But the patient owes certain duties to the doctor, as well as the doctor to the patient. This duty is defined by the word "trust." Let the sick man put entire confidence in his doctor; let him choose a doctor who is worthy of being a trustee; let him choose such a doctor before he becomes a patient. Choosing a doctor is the next most serious thing to choosing a wife; therefore, you should take time. Of course, also, as you choose the best woman you know to be your wife, you also will choose the best physician you know to be your doctor. Bear yourself toward your doctor in a manner of absolute trust; let him know you; tell him of your family, your ancestry, your history, constitution, habits; trust him with the secrets of your life. Many patients with their doctors, as clients with their lawyers or parishioners with their pastors, are not frank. When thus in health you have selected your doctor, make it your duty, as it is your right, to call him to your service. Do not let a sneeze be a signal for bringing him to your chamber at midnight, but remember that of the sickness which is the most serious, the first symptoms may be slight. When he is called, let your trust in him be complete; do not think that he will treat you too long, or call oftener than he needs; think that his interest is yours, your interest his. Do not dispute his bill; pay it. Love him.

Every doctor bears a relation to every other doctor. They are members of the same profession. What is this professional relation? What should be this professional relation? Important questions are these, and so important that I shall not venture to give an answer; but I shall venture to ask you to hear an answer made by one of the professors in this school. He says:

> Physicians' quarrels are proverbial, and have done much, perhaps most, to bring the profession under unfavorable criticism. The wherefore of

this is partly in the nature of their calling and is based upon the fact that you cannot create a demand for physicians. The supply is often ample when new candidates appear on the field for patronage. Another potent reason may be formed in the bitter feeling engendered in the heart of the physician, when old patients, who have been his warmest friends, and to whom he is strongly attached, are drawn away from him by the supposed greater merits of another physician. I mention these facts without designing to excuse this unfortunate, yet true, state of affairs. Young physicians, lately established in practice, often call upon me as a former instructor. I find, as a rule, they speak of the other physicians in their village, as "my opponent" and not as "my friend and colleague." This will explain to you the whole matter. Physicians are tempted to underestimate other physicians and overestimate themselves in the eyes of the people. Beyond other callings this is true.

This testimony is sad and saddening. Such manners may be consistent with professionalism of a certain sort, but they are not high and noble gentlemanliness. It is the duty of the doctor to be broad-minded, recognizing the professional merits of his brother physicians at their full value, giving to them that same quiet hiding of demerits which he desires to receive from them. Envy and jealousy are the temptations of the lawyer and of the minister no less than of the doctor; but to this temptation the members of your profession are to be unyielding. My own father, after hearing a young minister criticized in an adverse spirit by another minister, said to me, about to become a minister: "Charles, if you cannot say anything good about a brother minister, don't say anything." I may be suffered to adopt these words, and to say to you: "If you cannot say anything good about a brother physician, do not say anything." Let your silence be condemnation sufficient. It is always to be remembered that the lasso of depreciation, flung by the hand of jealousy to bring a rival low, often returns to ensnare him who flings it. Appreciation of a brother is eulogistic of him who appreciates. You treat the children of your professional brother without a charge of money. Trust him without charging inability or incompetency. Every physician who is doing worthy work in worthy ways can well afford to be generous toward every other physician. Be free from pettiness; enter not into the associations of the profession in the spirit of rivalry; be generous not in narrowness but in large wholesomeness; let the doctor bear himself as Christian, humane, human.

It is probable that the doctor is more a doctor than the lawyer is a lawyer, or the minister a minister. He is more professional. His profession is the most absorbing profession; his work is never done: he is busy when other men rest, he works when other men sleep. But he recognizes that even his profession does not free him from certain public duties. Doctors should take an active part in all affairs relating to the health of the people; they should recognize their duty as public guardians of important public interests. The modern city is a collection of disease germs. The modern physician should be as eager to prevent as he is to cure disease. In the present social agitation, too, he may play a most important and a unique part. Every great city has what is called its dangerous classes. They are composed of those whose hand is against law and order and against the property of its citizens. If they are not anarchists, their tendencies are anarchical. The ordinary minister cannot reach them; they look upon the church as the ally of capital; ordinary philanthropic movements awaken their pity. But for the worthy doctor they have the heartiest welcome; he can go among them not only with safety to himself, but with benediction and healing to them; he can, through the skill of his services, assure them of the worthiness of his science and of the merits of his art; he can also by the strength of his bearing assure them that law and order are the safeguards of society; he can by the gentleness and helpfulness of his ministry strengthen their assurances that not hatred, but love, is the proper conservative force of human society.

Toward the public, also, the doctor owes a special duty in doing what he can to restrain any innate tendencies to the acceptance of quackery. The quack is the man who knows little, but pretends to know much; who plays on public or individual ignorance, who is insincere. But of the quack many are fond. I hardly know the reason for such fondness, unless it be the reason lying in what is called the fascination of a precipice; it is like seeing how far one can go near a peril without losing oneself. It is for the true physician to assure the people that there is no royal road from the miasmatic valley of illness to the ruddy heights of health. This road is not paved with broken bottles of "Safe Kidney and Liver Cure." The fences along the way are not built of empty boxes of "Beecham's Pills." The sides of the road are not planted with potatoes to be carried in the trousers pocket to keep off rheumatism, or with olive trees for making oil for anointing the sick. Every doctor to whom I speak should hold it an honor to do what he may to put down all quackery. Of course, in himself, he will have no such temptation to deception; he will never seem to know what he does not know; he will not drive through Ohio mud to give the impression that his business is great, and that, like the king's business, it requires haste; he will not, like Gil Blas, make his impression as a doctor more from the completeness of his chest of instruments or of medicine than from the thoroughness of his diagnosis. No one of you, I am sure, will be like the physician who, when asked what his "heart regulator" was made of, answered, "Of all the bottles on the top shelf of the store," and to the question, "What is your liver cure made of," answered, "Of all the bottles on the lower shelf." Be assured the public estimates you in the course of your long practice at your true value. You need have no fears but that justice will be done you; the people for a time may judge unjustly, but such injustice is temporary and local. They will call you by names that will indicate their judgments. Some of you they will call the "sphinx." They will study your face while in one hand you hold your watch and the other the wrist of the patient; but no mounting flush in your cheek, no quivering of an eyelash, shall indicate your judgment. No skillful questionings which they can make can draw from you the suggestions of your thoughts. Some of you the people will call the "ogre" doctor. Every patient has come to his last sickness; every case of the measles will probably result in consumption; your face is as long as the bedstead, and the shake of the head is as ominous as the blackness of a cyclone. Some of you they will call the "fuss-budget" doctor, who investigates all housekeeping arrangements, giving minute details for toasting a piece of bread, or preparing a mustard plaster. This doctor has a dog's scent for smells, and a czar's method in ordering the daily routine of the household. Some of you they will call the "pussy-cat" doctor, who is comfortable, and makes everyone else feel comfortable; who carries a bag of candy in his overcoat pocket to give delight to the children and not to increase his practice. No sick man grows worse, but is as well as can be expected. If death does come, "Well, death has to come to every man some time, and this is the fullness of time." Yes, my friends, the people will classify you, giving you some name, which even if it attempt to be witty, is none the less wise and true.

I have so far spoken of the doctor in relation to his

patient, in relation to other doctors, and in relation to the people. I now beg your indulgence as I speak to the doctor in relation to himself.

To himself the doctor owes certain rights. He owes the right of continuance of the intellectual culture begun in the schools. This right gets peculiar value from the suggestive fact that only five out of every group of one hundred doctors in the country are college graduates. The bachelor's degree has no magic power. Some men secure a good intellectual training without the college. But it is at least true that the bachelor's degree represents the companionship of the best men, the reading of the best books, and leisure for high intellectual pursuits. The doctor who has not had this advantage should possess every means for making good this lack. No one knows his professional work unless he knows much more than his professional work. Every young doctor not college-bred, and indeed one college-bred, would do well to pursue a rigorous and vigorous course of intellectual study, outside of his professional work. What could be more advantageous than a thorough study of the best books in psychology? But above all, the physician is to keep all his faculties alert to see, strong to comprehend, exact to judge. His need is as great as that of the criminal lawyer, the need of the power of questioning his patient. He is to discover the whole truth, or at least the essential truth. Every case presented to him demands the mental grasping together into one idea of a multitude of minute details. Every case demands careful comparison, accurate weighing of evidence. Every case demands at an early stage application of a certain method of treatment. When I was a junior in college, Professor Child assigned to the class as a subject for writing, "The Uncertainty of Medicine." No one knows better than a doctor how uncertain is medicine; how uncertain is the wisest diagnosis; how uncertain is the effect of remedies. I know of a doctor who once boldly remarked, "No one of us knows what we shall find when we cut into a person," but so sharp should be the inner eye and so true the outer, that medicine should cease to be uncertain. The broad culture of the doctor insures to him a high standard of intellectual attainment. Let no new and worthy idea be whispered but that his ear shall hear and his brain profit by it. Growth depends largely upon entering into the new intellectual life of the age. Subscribe for the medical journals; write for them; read the newest and best books. The purse is small, but buy the new book even if you must ride in the rickety rig or wear the old coat. By and by work will be exhausting to intellectual vigor, but fail not to be a student. Be a student, young doctor, until you are fifty, and culture, growth, prosperity are assured. I may also be suffered to add, come back to this school and take some special or post-graduate course which these able and distinguished professors are happy to offer.

To his emotional nature quite as much as to his intellectual, the doctor owes certain rights. His appetites, desires, and affections are to be held in fitting adjustment. These springs of action are to send forth large and pure streams of noble conduct. The doctor is more tempted in his feelings than any other professional man. These emotional chords which make up so much of life's music easily get out of tune. The doctor sees the weak side of people; he is, therefore, tempted to lower his own standards of strength. The doctor sees the result of sin even more closely than the minister. He is, therefore, at times, tempted to yield to moral baseness because of association; as he is also to be strengthened, seeing the results of sin, against personal degradation. The doctor sees much of human brutality; he, therefore, is allured either to oversensitiveness or to undue hardness of heart. The doctor is tempted to make sickness his point of vision for beholding humanity. As a specialist sees the patient from the point of his specialty, so the doctor is prone to see all men in the pale light of sickness. The temptation is inevitable; but the temptation is to be overcome. Nature designs every human being to be well. Nature struggles to make and to keep every being well. Nature uses her wonderful power of adjustment to maintain health. Nature even takes care that men with one lung, and men with bullets in their backs, and men with indentations in their skulls, shall live and work, so great are her recuperative powers. Therefore, keep your body, your constitution, healthy, in order that you may be healthful. Let the doctor, as he becomes familiar with the scenes of suffering, beware, lest he grow hard-hearted. He is to grow in strength and robustness of heart. I know very well that the first sight of blood may have made you faint. I know distinguished doctors in this city, who, when students, became unconscious in the presence of the first operation they beheld. All such feebleness must pass away; the doctor must be strong, virile. He must be strong, not in indifference or hardness, but in the mustering of his desire and power to give help and health. As the years come in which every day will be filled with the associations of suffering, it will be a happy fortune if your will and power to give relief become the stronger and more sufficient, without your heart hardening into iron. A happier fortune it will be if your sense of power to give relief becomes so mighty, and so satisfying to yourself, that even the agonies themselves become less poignant. Such a process, I think, was in the life of the blessed Healer, Jesus Christ. The agonies and the woes, the weaknesses and the sicknesses, the bruises and the afflictions of fallen humanity, He felt and felt keenly; but He also felt and more keenly his power to bless. So deeply felt may be this power of blessing that the agonies and the woes, the weaknesses and the sicknesses, the bruises and the afflictions, shall cease to be dull throbs of grief, and become mighty inspirations to healing.

The doctor owes to himself a yet further right—the culture of his religious nature. Is the doctor tempted above other men to neglect this culture? Doctors themselves differ. One says, "The study and practice of medicine are toward a materialistic conception of man." Another says, elaborating the same idea, "The tendency is to believe that there is nothing in the human body that cannot be found with the scalpel or the microscope." Other doctors give a wholly different answer. One says, "The study of the human frame with its marvelous adjustments points to a personal God." Another says, "The contrast between the man dead and the man alive is so mighty that I infer that man is something more than dust." Another declares: "In my opinion, it is untrue—as it is sometimes charged—that a large proportion of physicians are atheists. There is nothing in the study or practice of medicine which should have any such a tendency." Thus, it is evident that upon doctors the study of the human body acts with that diversity of effect that an opiate works. The power or effect depends not simply upon the cause, but also on the material in which the cause works. For myself, I believe that the undevout doctor, like the undevout astronomer, is mad. As said a great French physician, who was an atheist, examining the human eye before his students, "Yes, gentlemen, there must be a God, but I hate him." Whether we hate him or love him, there is a God. It is the duty of the doctor to cultivate that part of his nature which bears relation to this God. This part is of course intellectual, emotional, ethical. In this culture, he is inclined to think he has not the advantages of other men. He believes himself to be cut off from attendance at church. I suppose that some doctors feel that they are absolutely debarred from what we call the privileges of worship in the church, on the Sabbath. I shall, therefore, beg leave to read you the testimony of one physician, a distinguished member of this faculty:

> It is true, physicians must ever be more or less irregular in church attendance, but much can be done to avoid this if it be so desired. My own experience has shown this clearly. I have been practicing medicine twenty-four years, and for the past fifteen years, have certainly been as busy as the average physician. And yet, in consequence of early habits inculcated, and a full appreciation of the value of church attendance, I found it possible to be as regular an attendant on the services, as most men of the congregation. It is true, this has been accomplished by persistently determining to give myself this benefit, by arranging my Sunday work in accordance, and sometimes at a pecuniary loss.

So also it may be said that at times it becomes the duty of the doctor to exercise the functions of a clergyman. The same professor, from whom I have quoted, says:

> It is no part of a physician's duty to thrust his religious belief upon the notice of his patient. This is not only bad policy, but worse taste. It is the duty of a physician to respect the religious belief of his patient, and I have considered it my duty at various times to baptize the children of Catholic mothers before sacrificing them or taking

> the risk of doing so. This all I have done with no appreciation whatever of the ceremony at such a time, but simply because the belief of the mother required it, and, it gave her comfort of mind and injured no one.

Thus, for the sake of those whom he serves, and also for his own sake, the doctor is to keep his better nature open toward his God.

In a word, the doctor owes to himself the duty of being the largest, truest, best, purest, noblest man. He owes to himself the duty of pursuing the highest ideals in a way most righteous; in seeking noblest results by the wisest methods; in attaining the best character by the securest agencies; in winning the finest skill for use in meeting human needs. He owes to himself, as he owes to humanity, of which he is a brother, and also to his God, of whom he is a son, to secure the richest and best that can be gained. To his own self he is to be true, and thus it follows, as the day the night, he cannot be false to any man, much less to his God. When the doctor at last comes to that end toward which every human being hastens, and from reaching which no power, however powerful, no skill however skillful, can lastingly restrain us, it will be a satisfaction to him, richer than gold to the merchant or fame to the author, that the misery and sorrowing, which go up from this suffering globe as it rolls along, are a little less terrible than when he wrote his first prescription. It will be the deepest peace to his soul, that for darkness he has shed light, for weakness given strength, and for sickness brought health.

Gentlemen of the Western Reserve Medical School, I congratulate you upon your future. In it I bid you Godspeed.

XV

THE MINISTRY FOR TO-DAY[1]

An assurance was given from Heaven unto the disciples of Christ immediately after Christ's ascension that they should be witnesses of him, even unto the uttermost parts of the earth. That assurance these disciples, becoming apostles, made real, for in three hundred years they had transmuted the Roman Empire into a Christian Empire. Gibbon, in a famous chapter, indicates his interpretation of the five great causes of the progress of the Christian faith through the Roman world. These causes, in the thought of the great interpreter, are found at once in the content of the message, and in the condition of the Roman world to which this message went.

For ourselves, to-day, those causes have their own special significance. To me, that significance relates to the opportunities, the conditions, in the world, and particularly in the American world, which make for the progress of the Christian faith, and which also make for the effectiveness of the Christian ministry. Those opportunities and conditions become causes. There

[1] Anniversary address delivered before the graduating class of the Theological Seminary of the Reformed Church in the United States, Lancaster, Penn., May 11, 1910.

are several of these causes. I wish to name seven. In turn I shall try to indicate how these conditions become causes, helping to make the Christian ministry effective.

The American world to-day is a world vastly interested in life. There never was a time when humanity was so interesting to humanity as the present. One cannot forget the old line of Terence, borrowed from the Greek—that nothing is foreign to one which belongs to mankind. To-day mankind is interested in mankind, and never so widely or so deeply interested as at this very hour. Open your paper to-morrow morning and the world lies before your eyes: a famine in India, a riot in China, an assassination in Egypt or in Russia, a crisis in England, the death of a sovereign—all the world lies before each of us with each sunrising. Humanity interests humanity. And in particular, friends, American life is of interest to us because American life is so imperfect. America is still in the making. Henry James, in his *Life of Hawthorne,* writes of America as having no Norman castles, no Middle Age cathedrals; and of American life as being, on the whole, very stupid. Matthew Arnold said that America was very uninteresting. America is uninteresting in respect to a historic past, in regard to many achievements; but America is, to every vital man, profoundly interesting for that very reason, because it is so imperfect, because her past lies in her future. Her future is not conjugated in the past tense.

America has become vastly interested in life; but,

also, America is greatly interested in truth. There never was a time, I think, when the pursuit of truth was a quest followed so urgently as at this hour. You may go to the biologist's laboratory, you may go to the astronomer's observatory, the minutest forms of life are to the one the object of his quest, the most remote stars are to the other of controlling absorption. You may go to the manufacturer's office, or to the workshop of the mechanic, and each is interested in the minutiae of the truth of his careful pursuit. Truth, truth, truth —is still, and is ever to be, one of our great quests. The word *veritas* or the rising sun is the most common part of the shield of the American college. Truth, everywhere, the American recognizes as our increasing and absorbing interest.

There is a third fact, too, by way of interpretation, that seems to me significant. It is the fact that the world is becoming a world of force. The old relation was static, the new dynamic. Henry Adams told me a few years ago that he had been plotting out the increase of horsepower in the world in the last centuries. Go back four hundred years and the amount of horsepower in the world was small. Every centennial and every decennial have brought forth a marvelous increase, and if the condition could be embodied in an arc of a small circle in the early time, at present the curve becomes a parabola, and he said to me in his characteristic way, "If we keep on increasing the horsepower in the world at the present rate, the world will go off into the everlasting bow-wows." The amount of force in the world has become tremendous, and is becoming still more and more tremendous.

There is a fourth fact that seems to me of some worth in our interpretation. It is this: America is a unique combination of materialism and idealism. On the face of things America is a most materialistic nation. The intimation I have given of the increase of force embodies and illustrates this remark. The delight we have in the things we touch, in the things we see, in the things we taste, in the things we feel, represents this great fact. America is called a nation of sensualism, of materialism, and the remark is true; but with the remark there is at once to be linked the further interpretation that America as seen beneath that surface is a nation of idealists. We believe, as I have said, in truth, and the quest of truth is the quest of the idealist. We believe, as I shall presently say, in the right, and the quest of the right is the quest of the idealist. We believe in the unseen, in the unheard, in the untouched, and in the eternal. There never was a nation that believed in its heart of hearts so profoundly in the greatest, in the eternal, in the universal truths and principles, as the American. Our benevolence represents idealism. Our great corporations embody an idea that becomes an ideal. America is more truly a nation of idealists than of materialists.

Furthermore, we in America are seeing a greater respect for man as man, and a diminished respect for the profession or for the occupation of the man. I speak to you who are going forth as clergymen; I speak to you, my brothers of the ministry, and my fathers; our profession is regarded less highly than in the olden time. I, for one, have but a small care for the respect paid to the "cloth." I do care, and care profoundly, for the regard for the man beneath the cloth. And America has the greatest respect for the man, for the man fine, noble, pure in heart, clean in morals, large in intellect, rich in character. But, if character be unworthy, however worthy the profession may be, there results despising for the man himself.

I intimated, also, that America is coming to have a deeper respect for right as right. I like to recall those words of John Stuart Mill in which he said, "If to hell I must go for doing right, to hell I will go." Right, first and foremost; and right, also interpreted by the rational understanding, by the highest and most accurate reason of man is primary. Right represents the quest of the American people as never before. President Roosevelt gained his power over the American people and over the world largely by his insistence upon simple righteousness. The laws passed by Congress, enforced by the Executive—laws touching rebates, laws touching pure foods—are simply illustrations of the increasing respect for simple righteousness. My friends, with all our chicaneries, with all our wrongfulness, the American people were never so thoroughly in earnest about righteousness as at this very hour.

Furthermore, there has been, I think, a large increase in respect to our interpretation of the naturalness of religion. Did not a church father say that every man is naturally a Christian? Every man is naturally religious. Into the content of the word we may breathe or on it put different meanings, but man must believe, and believe increasingly, in religion. One hundred years ago Fichte was preaching his doctrine of idealism; the ego was divinity. Presently Schelling came to preach his doctrine of correspondences as representing God. Hegel declaimed and reiterated his belief in pure being as standing for divinity. At almost the same time Schopenhauer affirmed his doctrine of the sovereignty of the will, the will standing for the absolute. In our time, Von Hartmann has preached the doctrine of the unconscious as representing God himself. Fichte with his ego, Schelling with his correspondences, Hegel with his pure being, Schopenhauer with his will as the chief thing, and Von Hartmann with the unconscious, represent the necessity of some religion for man. There has passed away the old, blatant affirmation of the negations; there is coming in a doctrine of the agnostic, of knowing nothing; but even this is passing away. Man is coming to believe in something, it may be the unknowable, but a something, or a somewhere, or a somehow. It may be a power, either personal or impersonal, that makes for righteousness, but a power men are coming to believe in. Religion is being received by the American people as natural for the natural man.

Now, if these conceptions have in themselves any truth at all, they open I think, my brethren and my fathers, a very wide door of service for the Christian ministry to-day. They open, I believe, the widest door that ever has been opened to the Christian ministry. The ministry represents life; the ministry represents a message from God, the Author of life. That message is conveyed by life. A message thus born, a message thus conveyed, makes the mightiest appeal to a nation and a world supremely interested in life itself. If life were not interesting, if life were commonplace or stagnant, or dead, of what value could be the message, of what worth the messenger? Because life is so fraught with interest, that door is wide open for you who bear the message. I think of one whom I heard preach, as a college man, for seven years—Phillips Brooks. How full of life was that great soul! And how full of life were the souls to whom he ministered according to their capacity and their yearning for larger forces. Phillips Brooks was a man of life to minister to life.

And also the minister bears the message of truth. He is convinced in intellect and conscience, and quickened in heart by this assurance. He has fought his doubts and gathered strength, assuring himself of the truthfulness of truth. He has a warm welcome for a world that is interested supremely in truth. If you, my brethren, if we, fathers, are ourselves possessed of truth, we shall find the world with ears open and heart responsive to receive it.

And, furthermore, this world of force has a great welcome for the ministry of force. Not a fugitive and cloistered virtue, but a virtue vigorous, outstanding, forth-putting, progressive, conquering. For that virtue of force the world has heartiest welcome. You have in yourself no power of intellect or of conscience, or of will, no power but that the world will stretch out its hand to link hands with you. If you are weak, the world has no place for you. Thank God you are strong!

The ministry, moreover, is a ministry of idealism, the idealism of a belief in God. The Christian faith is the profoundest type of an idealistic philosophy. You have in your soul, you preach with your lips, the belief in God; you have in your soul, you preach with your lips, a belief in the Divine and the human Christ—the Christ the first in time and in significance of all idealists. You have in your mind and you preach with your lips the belief in the Holy Ghost, unseen, spiritual; that belief embodies the highest type of the idealistic faith. You stand for the noblest type of idealism; you are idealists, and the world, in its heart idealistic, is a brother with you in your quest and in your service.

Furthermore, I rejoice that so many to-night can go forth, not first as ministers, not first as laying upon themselves certain professional obligations, but first as men. I have known many great ministers. I have known William M. Taylor, for so long a time among the greatest preachers of New York; I have known Richard Salter Storrs, whose lips were touched with the eloquence of Chrysostom; I have known, as I said, Phillips Brooks. Those men were great as ministers because they were greater as men. I care little, I hope I care properly, for the vows of ordination. They are sacred. Let not my words be at all interpreted as seeking to depreciate the great worth of these sacred vows. But, my friends, first and foremost be great souls, and in your great-soulness the world has a great welcome for you.

Also, in particular, I rejoice that the principle of righteousness is primary. "Is it right?" you ask yourself; and that primary question is more primary than any question regarding the method of divine existence, regarding the inspiration of the Holy Scriptures, regarding any theory of future rewards or punishments. Apply that single principle of your character to life, and life will rise with its glad acclaim to welcome you as happy and efficient coworkers.

Moreover, the minister of to-day meets the world desiring and knowing and appreciating the naturalness of religion. The heart yearns for religion, and the heart yearns more, and most of all, for the Christian religion. The heart yearns, too, for the minister of this religion. Let us give full value to the so-called non-Christian faiths. I have prayed in the temples of Buddha to the Christian God. I, a Protestant, have prayed in the cathedrals of the Roman Catholic church. I have prayed with you in God's first temples, the groves of spring time; but for the religion of our faith, the world, I believe, has a heartier welcome than for any other form. Our faith and our ministry affirm that God is the great *I Am;* our church and our ministers believe that God exists as Father, as Son, as Holy Ghost; our church believes and our ministry affirms that God is pure Being; our church believes and our ministry declares that God is will, is force, is power, is omnipresence; and our church believes and our ministry affirms that God exists apart from human interpretation or understanding, and that He is also immanent in His universe. Our Christian faith, embodied in this church and ministry, fullfils the demands for a natural religion. You have that faith for which the world, in her heart of hearts, yearns, for which the world, with reverent lips, prays.

And now, friends, who are the men, what is the type of minister that can fittingly embody and present and project these great qualities to meet the conditions of life? There are, it seems to me, four elements that must be incarnated in each soul. The first is greatness of intellect. By an intellect great, I mean an intellect able to think, I mean an intellect rich in knowledge, I mean an intellect able to reflect, to compare, to infer, to weigh evidence, to judge. The minister who can think has a great place awaiting him. Never be afraid, of course, of your thinking. Think, think, think! Think God's thoughts after Him, and the thoughts will lead you and your people to God, the Omniscient, All-thinking One.

A second characteristic is purity and warmth of heart. By warmth or purity of heart, I mean love. Every minister must be a great lover. He must have in himself the element of the father and the element of the mother. You can never love a church too much. If you love a church with all the power of your heart, you will find the members of the church becoming the children of God Himself, who is Love.

A third element is allegiance to an enlightened conscience, to the principle of right that you are to incarnate. The conscience is to be enlightened with all the truth that you can summon; and then, thus enlightened, it is the voice of God in your soul. Hear it. Obey its commands.

And the fourth and the last quality that I shall refer to, as to be found in this minister who thus may meet the world, is the quality of will. Strength of character is primarily strength of will. Great men have great wills; but those wills are guided by intelligence and quickened by love. Have great force in yourselves; force of body, force of every sort, to enlarge and to strengthen force of will. If, in yourselves, you are, according to all your capacity, large in mind, warm in heart, noble in conscience, strong in will, you are doing your part under God's grace to cause His church to become the greatest power in the world that either the world or the church has ever known.

I feel like offering to my younger brethren and to ourselves, fathers, a word of congratulation that we are called to the ministry in this day and in this America of ours. We sometimes speak of the church as declining, of the ministry as becoming weak. This charge, if there be any truth in it, is a charge based upon our misinterpretation of, upon our faithlessness to, our task. I think there never was a time when the opportunity was so wide, or the duty so binding, or the work so quickening as at this very hour. A few weeks ago I wrote to a dozen of the leading ministers in our country to-day, asking this question: "Do you think that the opportunity for the ministry is as open to-day as at the time when you yourself were ordained?" That note went to ministers in New York, Boston, and elsewhere, and from each one there came forth, without a word of exception or qualification, the great response: "The opportunity is more wide, the chance greater, than it was twenty, thirty, forty, fifty years ago." For you, men of any age and every age of service, the door is wide open: wide open for those who have feet to walk through. For you, for you, my friends, may grace be given to do all you can do to satisfy the hunger and the thirst and the need of this world of ours in this our day!

XVI

EMERSON'S PHI BETA KAPPA ORATION FOUR-SCORE AND TEN YEARS AFTER[1]

It is now fourscore and ten years since Ralph Waldo Emerson gave his oration on the "American Scholar." It was given before the Chapter of Phi Beta Kappa of Harvard College. The passing of the years has served to bring forth into fuller consequence and richer meaning this historic address. Its immediate result was, as said Mr. Lowell, a declaration of intellectual independence. Dr. Holmes and others have also added their testimony of its quickening worth.

The oration embodies, as is characteristic of Phi Beta Kappa addresses, both the permanent and the timely. Contrasted with other orations given earlier, such as Edward Everett's of 1824, or after, such as Charles Sumner's of 1848, such as Wendell Phillips' of 1881 on the "Scholar in a Republic," such as Woodrow Wilson's on the "Spirit of Learning," of 1909—great pieces of eloquent interpretation—Emerson's address of 1837 stands forth like a piece of Greek architecture, simple without bareness, massive without

[1] Delivered before the Phi Beta Kappa chapter of the University of West Virginia, and before other chapters.

congestion, beautiful without ornateness, full of lasting intellectual and ethical contentment.

On this occasion, therefore, may I beg your patience and gracious indulgence as I seek to point out the changes which the period of almost a century has wrought in the interpretations which Emerson gave?

You recall the general topic of the great oration: it is the influences which affect the American scholar. The question is what are the influences of which he is the object or the subject. Of these influences Emerson names three: nature, books, action.

Of nature Emerson says:

> The first in time and the first in importance of the influences upon the mind is that of nature. Every day, the sun; and, after sunset, Night and her stars. Ever the winds blow; ever the grass grows. . . . What is nature to him? There is never a beginning, there is never an end, to the inexplicable continuity of this web of God, but always circular power returning into itself.[2]

The significance of the eloquent and penetrating interpretations has become yet more significant with the passing of the decades. Nature has come to speak to the scholar, be he scientist or classicist, with a voice at once more informing, more inspiring, and more persuasive.

Nature has enlarged her created and creative forces. The astronomer has lengthened his eyeglass a thousand

[2] *Phi Beta Kappa Orations,* First Series, p. 26.

and more fold. His photographic plate has given to him stars which his unaided vision, or even his aided vision, could not see. At the other extreme, nature has given to the scholar worlds within the atom, or the electron, worlds well ordered, systematic, regular in movement, dynamic. From the infinitely great to the infinitely small, nature has endowed the scholar according to his capacity with her own limitless resources. Not simply nature which we call inanimate, but also nature vital has made contributions quite as wonderful and apparently as seemingly miraculous. In the character of her creative force, nature still refuses indeed to give up her eternal secret of origins. To go behind the first quintette of words of our Holy Scriptures, "In the beginning God created," has been found no passage. But with the assumption of life the scientist has given to scholarship the method by which nature develops her life: the method is from the simple to the complex, from the like to the unlike, from the so-called lower to the so-called higher, from the plant to the animal, from the animal to the human, and apparently from the human to the divine. In the laboratory of nature the scholar has gone back as an observer toward the beginning, and also as a prophet he has gone forward into the unknown. The words of the orator of ninety years ago have thus been proved to possess a significance richer and a meaning broader, deeper, higher, of relations more universal, than any seer would have dared to intimate.

A second resource of the scholar which our great

interpreter names is books. Of the worth or worthlessness of books pregnant words he speaks:

> The theory of books is noble. The scholar of the first age received into him the world around; brooded thereon; gave it the new arrangement of his own mind, and uttered it again. It came into him life; it went out from him truth. It came to him shortlived actions; it went out from him immortal thoughts. It came to him business; it went from him poetry. It was dead fact; now, it is quick thought. It can stand, and it can go. It now endures, it now flies, it now inspires. . . . Books are the best of things, well used; abused, among the worst. What is the right use? What is the one end which all means go to effect? They are for nothing but to inspire. . . . I would not be hurried by any love of system, by any exaggeration of instincts, to underrate the Book. . . . There is then creative reading as well as creative writing. When the mind is braced by labor and invention, the page of whatever book we read becomes luminous with manifold allusion. Every sentence is doubly significant, and the sense of our author is as broad as the world.[3]

How true and harmonious is the song which these apparently discordant notes sing! Yet indeed, notes more numerous and seemingly more dissonant has the history of the years brought forth. The book has become more important as a record, as an interpretation, as a poem, and as a teaching instrument. Archae-

[3] *Ibid.*, pp. 27, 28, and 30.

ology has become both a result and a cause inciting to further researches. In these ninety years, books, whose greatness is quite as impressive as their number is vast, have come forth in pregnant profusion and in massive procession. To call even their titles is eloquent. In the year 1837 Adam Smith's *Wealth of Nations* was almost the single authority in political economy. Mill's great work, so penetrating, so human, was yet to wait a decade for its publication. In 1837 Kant's Critiques were regnant, as they still are. The Scottish philosophy was also the chief teaching force in the university. Hegel was meditating his world systems. The later German philosophers of the absolute, Schopenhauer, Von Hartmann, Lotze, were yet to be. The whole psychological school lay in the dimness of a remote future. Macaulay was still serving as a judge in India; his history was to wait almost a score of years for its completion; Prescott was meditating his Mexico and his Peru; Motley his Netherlands; Parkman published his Conspiracy of Pontiac in 1851. Shelley, Byron, Keats had each died in the preceding decade. Wordsworth still lingered in the beautiful sunset of his long and peaceful day. But why go on? The quest is an unending one. The book as the inspiration, as the influence formative, as the resource of the scholar, has indeed vastly strengthened itself in the century. The scholar has learned to know some of its perils, and its limitations, but he has also learned its value as a tool, as an inspiration, as material for thinking, as a pile on which standing he may lift himself toward the overarching heaven. The library has indeed become, as Carlyle said, the university.

A third influence affecting the scholar is action. Of the value of action to the scholar our prophet says:

> I do not see how any man can afford, for the sake of his nerves and his nap, to spare any action in which he can partake. It is pearls and rubies to his discourse. Drudgery, calamity, exasperation, want, are instructors in eloquence and wisdom. The true scholar grudges every opportunity of action passed by, as a loss of power. . . . If it were only for a vocabulary, the scholar would be covetous of action. Life is our dictionary. Years are well spent in country labors; in town; in the insight into trades and manufactures; in frank intercourse with many men and women; in science; in art; to the one end of mastering in all their facts a language by which to illustrate and embody our perceptions. . . . The final value of action, like that of books, and better than books, is that it is a resource. . . . Character is higher than intellect. Thinking is the function. Living is the functionary. The stream retreats to its source. A great soul will be strong to live, as well as strong to think. Does he lack organ or medium to impart his truth? He can still fall back on this elemental force of living them. This is a total act. Thinking is a partial act. Let the grandeur of justice shine in his affairs. Let the beauty of affection cheer his lowly roof. Those "far from fame," who dwell and act with him, will feel the force of his constitution

> in the doings and passages of the day better than it can be measured by any public and designed display. Time shall teach him that the scholar loses no hour which the man lives. Herein he unfolds the sacred germ of his instinct, screened from influence. What is lost in seemliness is gained in strength.[4]

Such are the interpretations of limitless meanings, of infinite intimations, which our philosopher gives of the action which is the scholar's resource. It is an action which is both act and activity, but which also is more than either. It is the man living, sharing in all that belongs to humanity, forming an unlimited partnership with all men. It is the man choosing, the man doing and daring, the man suffering, tempted and triumphing, the man vital, vitalized, vitalizing. In these fourscore years and ten the field of action of the scholar has broadened unto endless horizons, has deepened unto unfathomed depths, has risen toward invisible zeniths. It has gone forth unto all races. It has promoted unity of man, and what is more essential, the unity of men. It has made the world a community. It has annexed China, Japan, India to the American neighborhood. It has carried all nations unto each and each unto all. Foreign tongues have ceased to be foreign; they have become native and vernacular. The movement has translated Virgil's *arma* into the word tool, machine. It has made the

[4] *Ibid.*, pp. 31, 32, and 33.

steel into instruments of infinitesimal precision and also into weights and forces colossal. It has sent the human voice over the mountains, across the plains, and under the oceans; it has taken Franklin's lightning and, throwing away his needless kite, has flung messages into space as though there were no space, and through time as if time were nought.

In the field human the scholar's action has become an even richer resource. To select only one field of achievement: the scholar, the American scholar, has fought greatest wars since Emerson spoke! The greatest civil, and the great international. In the year 1881 I heard Wendell Phillips give his oration at Harvard charging the American scholar with cowardice. Concerning the people's agitation for freedom for action, as well as for freedom for the slave, Mr. Phillips said: "Timid scholarship either shrinks from sharing in these agitations, or denounces them as vulgar and dangerous interference by incompetent hands with matters above them. . . . Pulpits, just so far as they could not boast of culture, and nestled closest down among the masses, were infinitely braver than the 'spires and antique towers' of stately collegiate institutions." [5] I also heard Charles William Eliot say at an hour following the oration in measured, low-voiced tones, "I appeal from the words of the orator of the morning to the green graves of the sons of Harvard fallen in the war for the preservation of the Union,

[5] *Ibid.*, pp. 200, 207.

for the freedom of the slaves."[6] The record written by the American Scholar with the pen dipped in his own blood in the years 1861-65 is eloquent of the action, patriotic and human, which belongs to the American scholar. A like eloquence is spoken, written in larger characters and on a broader page, by the quartette of years of 1914-18.

From this triangled field of influences, nature, books, action, Emerson passes over into the domain of the scholar's duties. In this domain he selects one as chief, the duty of self-trust. Of the faith which the scholar should have in himself he says:

> In self-trust all the virtues are comprehended. Free should the scholar be,—free and brave. . . . Brave; for fear is a thing which a scholar by his very function puts behind him. . . . The world is his who can see through its pretension. What deafness, what stone-blind custom, what overgrown error you behold is there only by sufferance,—by your sufferance. See it to be a lie, and you have already dealt it its mortal blow.[7]

The self-trust which our philosopher points out as a duty and as a right has been proved to be yet more of a right through the passage of the century. The ministrations of nature, the inspiration of books, the power of action have given to the scholar the right to trust himself with a confidence more thoroughly buttressed and more thoroughly founded. This self-trust

[6] In a personal conference and in correspondence.
[7] *Phi Beta Kappa Orations,* First Series, p. 36.

has become humble as it has become stronger, has become even more silent, save when its message needs to be heard, yet more active when duty calls, and still more aggressive when the voice within the bosom speaks its imperative. Enlarged and enlarging truth has vouchsafed to him its firmer support. The testimony of increasing ages has added evidence to and of his worth.

In the last paragraph of his immortal oration, Emerson says:

> The scholar is that man who must take up into himself all the ability of the time, all the contributions of the past, all the hopes of the future. He must be an university of knowledges. . . . This confidence in the unsearched might of man belongs, by all motives, by all prophecy, by all preparation, to the American Scholar. We have listened too long to the courtly muses of Europe. . . . We will walk on our own feet; we will work with our own hands; we will speak our own minds. The study of letters shall be no longer a name for pity, for doubt, and for sensual indulgence. The dread of man and the love of man shall be a wall of defence and a wreath of joy around all. A nation of men will for the first time exist, because each believes himself inspired by the Divine Soul which also inspires all men.[8]

The fourscore and ten years have brought new evidence of the truth of Emerson's words. These words,

8 *Ibid.*, pp. 41 and 42.

so clear, so penetrating, so inspiring, so persuasive, lift us, Emerson's children, to new levels of strength and to the promise of richest achievement. The days and the nights of the fourscore and ten years have uttered yet nobler speech and showed richer knowledge of the resources and duties of the American Scholar, because of Emerson's Phi Beta Kappa address of 1837.

XVII

THE RELATION OF THE COLLEGE AND UNIVERSITY TO THE COMMUNITY

Inaugural Address [1]

We are assembled, apart from the community, yet a part of it, citizens of a city, state, commonwealth. yet bearing peculiar relations to Adelbert College and to Western Reserve University. Therefore it is fitting for me to propose as the subject of our thought, "The Relation of the College and University to the Community."

The college and the university are intellectual, moral, spiritual forces. They are placed in a material world. Immaterial themselves, they cannot be worthy forces without material equipment. The more worthy their material equipment, the more adequate the immaterial results they achieve. This equipment they are themselves unable to make. No college supports itself. Every student is a beneficiary. The German university draws on the public chest. Oxford and Cambridge receive as the income of endowments more than three millions of dollars a year. The American college and university appeal neither to the national treasury nor to the gifts of an ancient past. They appeal to wealth

[1] 4th February, 1891.

personal and present. The voluntary principle is best in the American college as it is in the American church. It is as important for the university to be free from statecraft as it is for the church to be free from priestcraft, or the commonwealth from kingcraft. The college and university ask for material equipment. They found their demand upon reasons fundamental, substantial. They are the best trustees. No corporate institution, no individual, preserves funds so sacredly as the American college. Banks become bankrupt; railroads go into receivers' hands and stay there; commonwealths repudiate their bonds. No record of investment so secure and so remunerative does financial history show as that contained in the history of the older and abler college. The oldest college in America has funds that for more than two hundred and fifty years have given beneficent service, and which will continue to give this service so long as money may be transmuted into character. Capital finds no safer security than is represented in a college vault.

It is also to be said that funds given to the college and the university are of comprehensive beneficence. Mr. Matthew Vassar, considering the devise of his fortune, determined early to found a hospital. Later he did found a college. Founding a college, he founded a hospital, for a college extends hygienic knowledge. Funds given to the college are funds given to the cause of art. For without that culture which the college quickens, what is art other than mere manual dexterity? Yet, from noble culture art springs forth, giving to the canvas life, and to the marble breath. Funds given to the college are funds given to the church and to the cause of missions. For what is the church at home or abroad without a ministry, and what is a ministry without a college? Funds given to the college are funds given to the promoting of profoundest influences —character over character—in formative periods, at the springs of being, as lasting as the human soul.

The selfward motive has proper place. The names of our colleges are our Westminster Abbey, treasuring the memory of those who have wrought righteousness in noble beneficence. Whether he be John Harvard, who gave a few hundred dollars and a few hundred books, or Johns Hopkins, who gave seven millions; whether he be Governor Yale, who gave a wooden dormitory, or Ezra Cornell, who gave of his munificence; whether he be Lord Dartmouth, endowing an Indian charity school, or Amasa Stone, who gave a half million and more, no name is more certain of being spoken by men's lips than the names of those who are immortalized in beneficence to the American college. When the monumental marble has crumbled, men will still speak with admiring and reverent gratitude of George Peabody, Henry W. Sage, Joseph E. Sheffield, Jennie McGrew Fiske, Sophia Smith, John C. Green, and Price Greenleaf. Nor, when it is called to their remembrance, will they be less grateful to those who, in the spirit of the poor widow of the gospel, brought their silver spoons and gold cups to the college treasury, as was done at the founding of Harvard, that the altar of learning and of piety might not lack even the turtle dove of a not unworthy sacrifice.

Let it also not be forgotten that, if the college and university have large need of the wealth of the community, this wealth has yet larger need of the college and of the university. Without the aid of the higher education in the past, much of wealth could not have been created; and without the aid of the higher education of the present, wealth would now become sordid. Gold dust is no less dust because it is golden. The rich man needs the college as his beneficiary to help him to be a noble man quite as much as the college needs his benefactions to help it to make noble men. A college in poverty can make man; a rich man (or a poor man, indeed) cannot hoard in meanness without degradation in manhood.

Men, also, are not to fail to remember the wisest methods of beneficence. They are to give not only in generosity of amount, but also in freedom of conditions. Let them trust the college not only with money, but also with the best use of the money; let them credit the college with having not only an honest treasurer, but also a wise executive. Let not a dead hand forever rule. Benjamin Franklin was the wisest American of his time, and generous; but bequests he made to education are already in part valueless by reason of the conditions attending them. What sort of a world the sun of the morning of 4th of February, 1991, may rise upon no prophet dare intimate. Let wealth not forget, too, that to itself it owes somewhat in the enjoyment of the giving, and also in the result of giving. He who has the joy of amassing should not suffer himself to lose the joy of distributing. Wealth is not a diamond to be treasured, but a seed to be planted, to die; through death to gain a broad and lasting life. "Of all your work, what have you enjoyed the most?" was asked George Peabody. "The lodging houses I built for the artisans of London." The poor boy of Dunfermline, who has become the great steel-maker of the world, preaches and practices on two continents the gospel of beneficence in one's lifetime. Funds given by the living hand are safe; funds given by the dead hand are not so safe as some colleges wish they were.

The colleges and universities offer opportunities for gifts large and small. They receive one dollar and put it to its designed and effective uses; they receive the million and ask for more. They are like a bank in willingness to receive; they are unlike a bank in not having remunerative funds—on deposit. The treasurer of Adelbert College was recently informed of a bequest, made by a young graduate, of one hundred dollars; when received, it will at once begin its blessed transmutation into disciplined character. In the decade just closed, this college and university have received more than a million dollars, all of which is also daily passing into the imperishable treasures of the human mind and heart. In this new decade the institution should receive a second million, that it may be adequately equipped for doing its large and enlarging work. Its library now needs at least fifty thousand dollars for the purchase of books. A university is, in no small degree, a collection of books. Its laboratories and museums need a hundred thousand dollars for their better housing and provision. Each of several professorships, in the college for men and in the college for women, calls for fifty thousand dollars in endowment. Its art school needs fifty thousand dollars for a building, for which a site is provided. Its school of medicine, admirably equipped for service in its new building, calls the more loudly for endowment. Its school of music is in need of proper halls. And its academies ask for foundations that they may do the better their important work in a part of the country where first-rate fitting schools are sorely lacking. These are a few of the needs of this college and university. They are needs that must be met. Some are to be met this year, some the next, and some the following. Large needs they are, and they are to be met by largeness in supply. They are to be met, in no small part, by the citizens of a city of nearly three hundred thousand people, which is by ratio of population and wealth the richest American city. For its unexampled heroism in defending itself in its unexampled siege, Leyden was offered by William of Orange a reward. The great stadtholder, so runs the story, gave the city the choice between freedom from taxation and the establishment of a university. The citizens, wise as they were brave, chose the university. To the citizens of Cleveland, city of riches, city of learning, a kind providence offers the choice of wealth larger by a small addition and the choice of a college and a university most worthy. This city has become conspicuous by the richness of treasures it has dug from the earth. Let this city become also conspicuous by loving and glorying in an institution where the treasures of knowledge may be mined, where the lasting ideals of truth, honor, virtue, may be upheld, where leaders may be trained for the people, where the people may learn righteousness, where the black coal of human nature may be transmuted into the lustrous diamond of white character, and where manhood may be tempered to become as strong as iron and as firm as steel. This city has become conspicuous in having as its chief thoroughfare an avenue which a world traveler calls the most beautiful that the foot of man treads. For its sloping lawns and its arching elms are a park, and its houses are palaces. Let this city also become conspicuous in that this same avenue, as it goes toward the sunrise, has on its right the clustered buildings of its college for men, and on its left the noble foundations of a noble college for women, where manhood may make itself pure and womanhood may make itself strong; and where both manhood and womanhood may be cultured for the serving and the saving of humanity and for the glory of God. I have no doubt that the choice of Leyden, small, poor, brave, and wise, in the little republic of the old world, will be the choice of Cleveland, large, rich, earnest, wise, in the great Republic of the new world.

If to the more material forms of the common life the college and university hold intimate relations, to that form which is least material they also hold relations no less intimate. Close relations learning and Christianity have held for all the Christian centuries. The greatest of the apostles of Christ was a student of one of the greatest of Jewish teachers. For a thousand years the only educated man was the priest, and the only college the monastery. The first American colleges were founded to train ministers. The lamp of learning is fed by the olive oil of piety; but olive trees grew in Athens as well as in Gethsemane. The Christianity which became incarnate in the college is fundamental in principle, essential in meaning, broad in application. The denominational college is loyal to a denominational interpretation of Christianity—all honor to it. The Christian college is loyal to Christianity itself. It has no lack of piety because of a lack of ecclesiastical affiliation. Its piety is the more vital because its relation is the closer to Him who is life eternal; its lamp of truth is the more radiant because lighted by Him who called himself the light of the world. It is the more intent to follow the divine and human light for its guide, as it has a clearer vision of Him who is "the Truth." It can be the more loyal to Christ, and the more useful to men, as it is lifted above dependence on arbitrary relations. The great college and university are to be as free from denominational control as they are to be pervaded with the spirit of Christianity. They are to be as true to the truth of the gospel as they are to be remote from schismatical partisanship. In aim the college is to be Christian; perfection: "Be ye therefore perfect even as your father which is in heaven is perfect." In method and agency the college is to be Christian: the power of personality: "And I, if I be lifted up . . . will draw all men unto me." In motive the college is to be Christian: the love of God: "God so loved the world that he gave his only begotten Son that whosoever believeth in him should not perish, but have everlasting life." Its constitution is the Sermon on the Mount; its laws are the decalogue; its ethics are comprehended in the two great commandments; and its graces are pictured in the beatitudes. As said one of the greatest teachers, Mark Hopkins, on the fiftieth anniversary of his connection with Williams College: "Christianity is the greatest civilizing, molding, uplifting power on this globe, and it is a sad defect in any institution of high learning if it does not bring those under its care into the closest possible relation to it."

But more than to either the material or the ecclesiastical part, the college and the university hold relations to the people themselves. Every college, every university, is the child of the people. It is born among them, of them; it is christened at the public altar of a constitutional character. From the people the college receives its students. In this country about one person in each group of one thousand persons is a member of a college. In England not more than one person in every group of four thousand is a member of a university. In Germany one person in every group of two thousand is a member of a university; but the proportion in the gymnasium is much larger. The college is happier the larger the number of students it receives from the people. At Oxford and Cambridge five students of every six are sons of either the rich or of the clergy. In American colleges one student in every three is earning, at least partially, his education. To every boy and girl, poor in purse but rich in brain, the college holds open its great opportunities. To the people the college says, "Send us your best and we will return to you the finest character into which manhood or womanhood can flower." For it is to the people that the college and university desire to give more than they receive from the people. It is not unjust to say that the people are debtors. The community has given to Yale and to Princeton and to Harvard much, but Yale and Princeton and Harvard have given to the community more. For the college and the university are set to hold up the worth of things of the mind, and these things are the worthiest. In an age democratic and material they are to represent the monarchy of the immaterial. In an age of luxuriousness they are to declare the words of Him, homeless and pillowless, who said, "A man's life consisteth not in the abundance of the things which he hath." They stand for the continuity of the best life, intellectual, ethical, religious, Christian. In the realm of thought they stand for the value of ideas; in the realm of morals for the value of ideals; in the realm of being, like the church, for the value of character.

The college recognizes its duty to the present. It is training men and women for service in the fifty years—1891-1940. It can do the most for the first decade of the twentieth century by doing the most for the last decade of the nineteenth. Its various agencies are adjusted to immediate conditions. Its culture is therefore vital. If it looks into the past—and into the past it must look—it looks, like the oarsman, that it may secure a course more direct in present and future achievement. The scholar should make all antiquity a prophet for to-day, as Grote made his history "a modern political pamphlet in twelve volumes." The college should fill that dire need of the new world of wise leadership. It should train every faculty in every man unto effective and gracious facility. It should cause noble character to blossom in noble doing, as noble doing is the seed of yet nobler character. It should not, or it cannot, dictate legislation, but it should fit men to become worthy lawmakers. It should not, as it cannot, step over the threshold of domestic rights, but it should so train women that they, in wifehood and motherhood, may worthily train the generations to be. It should not stand blindfolded as justice and mute as the Sphinx before terrible social problems, but its eye should discover ways of relieving the increasing wants of suffering humanity, and its voice should be a bugle in clearness and a flute in sympathy, calling man to help man. Its interests are humane because they are human. It teaches a love of one's country, of one's world, of one's God.

The agency by which the college and university seek to render these services to the people is their students. For training their students the college and university need time, but time is a condition, not an agent. The question of the length of the college course is not of the first importance. If a student may secure competent training for life's work in three years, or even two, let him not spend four. If he cannot secure this training in four, let him not hesitate to spend five. Shorten the college course, lengthen the college course, but train the college man for life and for living. In the training of students the college has used Latin, Greek, mathematics—admirable agencies for many men, for some men not the best and not for them to be made chief. For some men, studies in science, history, philosophy, are more worthy. Each student should be trained by those agencies which will insure him the largest usefulness in the next fifty years. In the training of students the college has, or is, the teacher; the teacher represents truth in life and life through truth; both are applied in the power of his personality to the development of character. If the college serves the people through its graduates, these graduates are students who are molded by their teachers. If Rugby boys have helped to make modern England, Arnold made Rugby boys. The education thus received should be broad enough to allow it to be called liberal, but not so broad that, becoming thin, it deserves to be called superficial. The graduate should know enough about some things to deserve to be called thorough; he should know enough about all things not to deserve to be called narrow. The college is not to try to give the student such an education that it merits the charge of aiming at omniscience, as did the old college; but it is to aim to give him through knowledge such a training that he may respect himself, love his brother, honor his God.

By these agencies, under these conditions, the college is to reach the people. Discard Greek, but reach the people; retain Greek, but reach the people; shorten the college course or lengthen the college course, but reach the people; keep to the required system, but reach the people; introduce the elective system, but reach the people; keep out the sciences or let them in, but reach the people; bring in German methods, but reach the people; discard German methods, but reach the people. Let not the American college be obliged to offer excuses for its mere being because in its remoteness from the people it is so useless; rather let every American home be obliged to offer excuses for not sending its sons and daughters to the college, because the college in its abounding usefulness is so near to the home.

Upon the altar of this college and university burns most radiantly the flame of the desire to serve the people. This institution wishes to bless this city, this state, this nation, this world. It has no prejudices to nurse, no heresy to teach, no schism to perpetuate.

This college and university are for the people—not for the poor as poor, not for the rich as rich, but for men and women as men and women. They wish to bless this city; but they also wish to receive the blessing of this city. They wish to maintain in this many-college State a high ideal and a noble achievement of college and professional education; but they wish, as they have the right to wish, the expressed approval of the four millions of people of this State. Near the center of America's population, they wish to send forth into this great humanity the blood of clear thinking, pure feeling, noble doing. But they also wish, as they have the right to wish, to receive sustenance from every part of this body. To every agency like themselves they stretch forth a hand of heartiest coöperation. To every church of God among men they would display the shield of this ancient college an open book, truth borne upon a heart, love surrounded by the words, *Christo et Ecclesiae.* To man, to men, they give themselves.

In the power of God, under the symbol of the divine and human cross, this college and university thus devote themselves. When Perry was about to sail from a port on this lake, and bearing its name, to win the most famous naval victory ever won by us from foreign foe, he caused the figure of the cross to be raised above the streaming ensign, while the minister invoked the divine blessing and summoned sailors to do their duty. Unto untried waters, to meet unknown perils, this college and university move forth to-day. Upon this institution I invoke the benediction of God; for it I ask the love and aid of men; and above the treasures of its museums and libraries, above the lifted towers of its high scholarship, above, yet within sight of, its trustees, teachers, graduates, students, benefactors, and friends, I raise the figure of the cross, symbol of God's love for man, symbol of man's duty to himself and to his God.

XVIII

THE DEMOCRATIC PRINCIPLE AND METHOD IN COLLEGE GOVERNMENT

FAREWELL ADDRESS [1]

THE higher education, in these thirty years, has been favored in the rising tide of certain great human movements. If the interest of the people in affairs, philosophical and theological, has lessened, the interest of the people in education, general and particular, has advanced. The interest, too, in the charitable and philanthropic movements of society has become wiser and more commanding. Such interest and such conditions have promoted the development of this and of every other university. Be it also said that the growth of the city of Cleveland has strengthened the foundations for the University, foundations the value of which, at the present time great, will become greater in the future years.

In the recent weeks I have naturally reviewed somewhat the service which I have tried to give. My mind has rested largely on the principles and methods of this service, and on the persons with whom I have been privileged to serve. It is to these principles that I

[1] Extracts from address upon retirement from the office of president, November 11, 1921.

would call and keep your thought. As I seek to interpret them as belonging to the past, I find myself also in a mood somewhat prophetic.

The first of these principles—and in certain respects the most fundamental—is the principle of democracy. The government of American colleges and universities is easily divided into the two methods described by the words democratic and autocratic. The autocratic method is not so general as it is usually supposed to be. But it is more common than it should be. The autocrat in this autocracy is the president.

This autocracy is usually visible and audible in the selection and dismissal of professors. A most delicate process is such selection and dismissal, personal, sensitive, quivering with the whole life of the college. In contrast with such a method, the democratic principle has here prevailed. It has prevailed not by forceful demands made by earnest associates, but it has prevailed by spontaneous origins and grateful coöperations. The democratic method or principle possesses several advantages: (1) It commands the wisdom in legislation, and the coworking in administration, of many minds of diverse experiences. (2) It tends to lift the level of professorial interest from an absorption in a single department of study, or of teaching, to an interest concerned in all academic affairs. (3) It tends to remove personal professorial partisanship. (4) It gives a distinct quickening to the enthusiasms of the academic body, enthusiasms both intellectual and emotional. (5) It also promotes orderliness throughout the academic circle. It tends to dissipate revolts before they arise.

Yet, be it said, the democratic principle and method are subject to certain disadvantages: (1) The principle may prevent, or dissipate, initiative, dividing personal academic affairs among many, and too many, associates, lessening the sense of individual responsibility, retarding the beginning of reforms or of new movements. This disadvantage, however, is not inevitable and should not be natural. (2) It may tend, like all forms of democratic government, to result in compromises. Compromises in a university, as in other administrations, often represent a sacrifice of executive values to personal adjustments. (3) It may increase, in certain respects, the labor of the president. For it is easier to be an absolute academic monarch, or despot, than a constitutional president. It is to be said, however, that the constitutional methods may result in less ultimate toil and trouble. (4) It may also increase the less remunerative work of the college teacher and scholar. The college teacher holds the most important, serious, and commanding of all academic places. To request him to do executive work seems almost a degradation. It is the commanding of the priest of the altar to be an acolyte.

Disturbances, petty and transient, or insurrections indeed of serious nature, are not unknown in American college annals. They are, however, constituted, quite as often and quite as significantly, by the newspaper as by the academic conditions themselves. But not infrequently they do have a really significant cause. The formal teaching or the ill-considered, or unconsidered, comment on public affairs by a professor is the not unusual occasion of such academic disorder. But I do venture to affirm that such outbreaks are more prone to occur and to furnish more lively occasion for public discussion in universities in which the autocratic system prevails. The democratic system is indeed no assured panacea. But the democratic system does nourish the atmosphere in which disorders do not naturally arise. Democracy, moreover, is a better cure for the evils of ill-considered remarks than is autocracy. The interpretation is quite as true in academic, as in political or civil, circles.

There is one consideration in weighing the advantages and disadvantages of the democratic system which should not be passed over. It is found in the responsibility which the general community believes is vested in the president. Even if he have no power, the public believes that he does have it. Even if his power be only partial, the public believes, or is inclined to believe, that his power is absolute. If, therefore, the methods which are pursued be unwise, or if the conditions created for the college be unhappy, he is at once held to be the agent, and is often made the victim. He may, indeed, have opposed such methods and have sought to eliminate the undesirable atmospheres or conditions. Nevertheless, he is regarded as their author. Of course, such results are hard for him to bear. But bear them he must. On the other side, it is at once to be said that the public credits him with the laying of foundations, with the inauguration of new methods, with the creation of new and happy conditions, with which, perhaps, he has had no direct concern. His credit for such results he may justly regard as an offset to possible debits.

In the balancing of the advantages and the disadvantages of the democratic and autocratic systems of government, the weight of evidence, therefore, turns toward the democratic. Of course, it is to be said that an autocratic system may be so applied that it results in an essentially academic democracy; and it is also to be added that the democratic system may be so manipulated that it solidifies itself, for a time at least, into an autocratic. But I do believe I am not unduly straining your loyalty when I say that the democratic system in this university has been applied under a democratic belief and in a democratic spirit.

A second principle, derived directly from the first, of democracy, is the principle of freedom. For self-government is a free government. Freedom as applied in college concerns is the special right of the individual teacher. Under it, the individual teacher is allowed and required to be responsible for the conduct of his own department. It is indeed a dangerous method. It is a method fraught with many and diverse perils. But the opposite method of exterior direction is subject to perils even more numerous and more serious. But the perils, so far as human wisdom or power can repress or remove them, are eliminated by the selection of worthiest teachers. If professors worthy of confidence are named, qualified to bear their responsibilities, the whole delicate and complex problem is solved. Such freedom given to the individual teacher has several fundamental merits: (1) It tends to attract the best teachers to the college using it. (2) It tends to create and to nourish teachers who are worthy to use and to enjoy freedom of academic control. (3) It tends to give to the students a sense of responsibility for the worth of the department in which they are enrolled. A possible objection to the method lies in the peril of individual and professorial eccentricity. Independence easily becomes eccentricity. A professor may forget that he is a member of a body and that his work is to relate itself to and function with other parts of the academic system. The balance between the centripetal and centrifugal is to be heeded. It is thus that the academic solar system maintains its harmony. But the peril of eccentricity may in advance be removed by care in the original election. The success of freedom in a department of a college, or in the whole college itself, rests quite entirely on the wisdom of the electing body. The need, indeed, of wisdom in the electing body cannot be overestimated.

I am sure that the Western Reserve University of the next decades and generations will be a university in which democracy shall prevail as a directing method, in which freedom shall quicken the noblest scholarship and teaching, in which fellowship shall unite and inspire all for each and each for all, in which patience shall work her perfect work, and in which service for mankind shall quicken the understanding and move the imagination. New occasions will teach new duties. New duties will create new occasions. Both new occasions and new duties will reveal new truths, and new truths will make new men for the new world and for the new to-morrow. To these men, heartiest greetings! Farewell to the past, and to the future—Hail!

INDEX